I'M A DREAM GIRL

A Guide to Fulfilling Your God-Given Dreams

Makayla,

May all your dreams come true!
"Hope deferred makes the heart sick
but a dream fulfilled is a tree
of life." Prov. 13:12 NLT

Penne Allison
Penne Allison

Cover Designer: Michael Curwen of Backslant
Author Photo: Emerson Able III
Published by Penne Allison LLC
P.O. Box 15564, Savannah, Georgia 31416

This book is affectionately dedicated to my husband Steve and my son Benjamin. You both have been patient, kind and supportive as I have labored to birth my first book. Thank you from the bottom of my heart! I love you beyond anything you can imagine.

This book is also dedicated to every woman who will embrace her identity as a daughter of the Most High God and start to dream big dreams. For each lady who takes a risk, always remember to dream out loud and silence every dream killer.

WORDS OF GRATITUDE AND THANKS

All glory and thanks to God who made my life possible. I can do nothing without Him. My purpose is found in Him alone. He is the hope of my highest dream.

Special thanks to God for my parents: Mary and Malcolm Stewart who came together to produce me, who taught me, loved me, and supported me throughout my entire life. May they both rest in God's care.

My deepest appreciation to: my sisters Rosalind Able and Rhonda Jenkins; my nieces Emerald Able and Shannon Jenkins for being present for the first Dream Girl Retreat—your love and encouragement during my journey has been steadfast; my aunt Ruth Strong who taught me how to cook and how to be a "Dream Girl," and who has always been there for me.

Special thanks to some of the midwives who helped me take the Dream Girl Movement to another level: my ace supporter and friend Denise Brown-Henderson, Esq. of Oikeo; my editor Janet Talbert—your guidance and prayers for this project have been exhilarating, and I have learned so much from you; Dr. Claudette Anderson Copeland—you inspired me with an amazing, phenomenal foreword; my graphic designer Michael Curwen, who is a creative genius; my website designer Taccara Martin, you made the movement come to life. And much love to my marketing consultants and new friends Jean Riggins and Michele Bolden, aka "The Lunch Bunch."

Special thanks to the intercessors who have prayed for me and blessed my life over many years: Rosalind Able; Solar Akala; the late Elisabeth Ashton; Catherine Barnes; Ruth Ann Bertine; Holly Buford-Brack; Doreatha Carlos; Sandra Chambers-Reed; Marilyn Clark; JoAnn Clem; Donna Covington; Lavatrice Davis; Pangela Dawson; Linda Delaney; Michele Fabery; Cindy Hale; Beverly Hillman; Rhonda Jenkins; Toni Lucey; the late Diane Mason; Audrey Mathis; Veronica Miller; Renee Pryor; the late Cecilia Osbourne; Karyn Prince; Janet Reed; Karliss Quisenberry; Karen Riggs; Tijuana Stewart; Carole Strong-Thompson; Kathleen Tyehimba; Teresa Tyler; and Sharon Williams.

Special thanks to all the ministers who have influenced my life over many years: Pastor Samuel Ford; Pastor Alvin O. Jackson; Pastor Frank Thomas; Pastor Denise Bell; Pastor Bill Edwards; Pastor Thomas Murray; Pastor Melvyn Gross; the late Pastor Shirley Prince; Pastor Stacey Spencer; Pastor Lee I. Brown; Pastors Marion and Stephanie Dalton; Pastor Richard Gaines; Pastor Mike Robinson and Minister Erin Robinson; Apostles/Pastors Charles and Verdise Bradford; Pastors Corey and Tomekia Williams; Pastor Nadine Burton; Pastor Jackie McHenry; Minister Regina Taylor Osei; Apostle Nancy Franklin; Chaplain Sheryl Armstrong; Pastor Deborah Thompson; Prophet Anthony Avery; Apostle Randall Quisenberry; Pastor Phillip Anthony Mitchell; Pastor Reginald Strong; Pastor Jon Weece; Pastor Gary Black; and Pastor Stephon "Ray" Henderson.

Special thanks to my friends who have supported me through the years: Betsy Cannon; Thelma Fisher; Toni L. Fleming; Geneva

Simpson-Moore; Deborah Brown; Joe and Sandra Reed; Calvin and Linda Strong; Tina Jackson; Neal and Rosetta Beckford; Edith Kelly Green; Darryl and Stacie Arbor; Howard and Delisa Eddings; Shantel Ross; Sharon Bell; Patricia K. Howard; Matthew Proud; Colette and Obie Taylor; Martin Anababa; Leo Davis; Patricia Hayes; DeAnna McCallie; Jennifer Jenkins; Diana Weaver; Jamie Holmes; and Sonya Pickett.

CONTENTS

FOREWORD

"Now Joseph had a dream, and when he told it to
his brothers, they only hated him more…" Genesis 37:5

Dreams or illusions, call them what you will,
They lift us from the commonplace of life,
To better things. -- Henry Wadsworth Longfellow

Many church women have embraced the *narrow* God. We have tiptoed tentatively toward the God of roles, rules and rituals, and right and wrong. We follow the God who *frowns*. We have bowed to the God of structures and strictures; rehearsed practices and regulated existences. We have *reduced* God to the level of our own deflated dreams and disillusioning religious experiences. We search the landscape of "church life" to see if anyone else is alive, *really* alive, not just functioning.

And one day, we acknowledge the whispers at the outskirts of our days: *"There must be something more to life than this!"*

Yes, we have embraced the narrow God, and our lives have remained narrow. Barren. Tired. Dreamless.

Yet the happy paradox is this: We can wake up from the "nightmare of nothingness" and start dreaming, and creating, and participating in the *exhilarating* stuff *called LIFE!* We have discovered that in giving women a safe space (the retreat setting); competent spiritual direction; the emotional space to do their inner work under the "tent" of the Holy Spirit's operation, *awakening miracles* happen!

What might occur with a new vision of God? What might change the way we live if we saw God living within us in a brand new way? Do you know the God who smiles? Have you met the God who laughs? Who dances? Who taps His feet and claps His hands? Do you fellowship with the creative God, whose eyes twinkle with the wonder of an ever-unfolding creation? In other words, do you know the GOD WHO DREAMS?

Penne Allison offers us a thoroughly Biblical challenge to find courage to militantly assault the assassins of our highest aspirations, and to be the children of a dreaming God. This God has been dreaming eternal and magnificent dreams about us since eternity past. God has downloaded into us the DNA to materialize these dreams, and make them realities in the earth. In spite of the haters or the castigators, Penne urges us to take the risk. As it says in 1st John 4:17, "...as He is, so are we in this world." Dream Girls!

But we are not just to stop at being dream girls. We can become *winning women*, who contagiously spread our joy (to borrow a media phrase) at finally "living our best lives."

Penne Allison is that God-sent voice to make it so. She offers us a solid, scriptural and unapologetic push to unleash the dormant spiritual potential within our spirits. She reminds us to allow this power to overflow into our groggy souls and overworked bodies. She teaches the new Christian in digestible, concrete baby steps. She convicts the seasoned, mature Christian about the ways we have gone to sleep at the wheel and are careening on cruise control over the cliff of excuses.

When you take this treatise to heart, you will get busy gathering the right midwives to help you deliver your dreams into history. You will redeem the time you have left, and with every hour you will once again nudge your dreams to life.

Be still. Rest. Go all the way down to the still place, for we are not hypocrites in our sleep. Then in Dream Sleep, be transformed! Soon you will hear the ALARM CLOCK in your soul. Then wake up and work with the GOD who DREAMS bigger dreams for you. Come on now! Penne reminds us...our world is waiting!

Here's to Penne Allison's urgent message.

Here's to better things!

The Reverend Claudette Anderson Copeland, D.Min.
Pastor, New Creation Christian Fellowship, Windcrest, Texas
Director, WOMEN'S SPIRITUAL ENCOUNTER: Spiritual Acceleration Through Emotional Cleansing

I'M A DREAM GIRL

A Guide to Fulfilling Your God-Given Dreams

INTRODUCTION

In December 2006, I saw the movie *Dreamgirls* with some friends. I was taken by the music, the dancing and the storyline, and began to ask myself if the movie had any spiritual applications for my life. Then I realized that every woman I know has a dream, but for some reason many of those dreams were broken or deferred, and only a few of those women have ever fulfilled their dreams. Finally, it occurred to me that God is the giver of dreams and visions for our lives. For a dream to come to life, God has to be involved.

Back then, I lived in Lexington, Kentucky, and worked in an academic medical center as a nurse executive in emergency services. But after I'd had the revelation about the importance of dreams in our lives, I met with some close friends at a local restaurant and discussed purpose, destiny and the dreams God has put inside each of us. That dinner was the beginning of something wonderful! As I continued to meditate and think about dreams, I had a few more get-togethers in the spring of 2007. I continued to talk to my girl-friends about their dreams and what they believed the future held for them. For the final gathering I wanted a more intimate setting, so I cooked a delicious meal, invited over some friends and sat down again to discuss specifics around dreams, visions and destiny based on key scriptures.

The next morning, I got up and began to have some "quiet

time"—time alone with God. The most amazing thing happened! God spoke very clearly to me about a way to organize a Women's Empowerment Workshop based on dreams. He "downloaded" the titles of six sessions to me. I wrote them down as quickly as they came. I kept the thoughts close to my vest for a while, but I never let them go.

Shortly after I received that wonderful download from the Lord, I was asked to get involved in a leadership team at my church, so I put the Women's Empowerment Workshop on the shelf for an entire year. In the summer of 2008, I stopped serving on the leadership team and, as time allowed, I went back to working on the Dream Workshop idea once again, this time focusing on creating a curriculum.

The fact that I worked a full-time job in a busy, Level 1 trauma center presented me with some time challenges, but I felt an urgency to get the workshop completed, so I set aside time early in the mornings, late at night and on weekends. I enjoyed researching the project's main concepts, but the process was very time consuming. Nonetheless, I kept moving forward, and squeezed my schedule to the hilt. By the end of 2008, I had a good framework and conceptual model. I felt ready to share what I believed God wanted me to do and I also wanted to proceed with prayer, so I called on a few close friends who are praying women and intercessors. My wonderful friend Donna Covington opened her home and hosted the first prayer meeting. The marvelous ladies who gathered that night agreed to pray weekly for six weeks, and also graciously committed to help me put on the first Dream Girl Weekend. In the New Testament, the name Barnabas means "son of encouragement." These ladies were daughters of encouragement, and an incredible support to me.

On February 21, 2009, The Women's Empowerment Workshop/

Dream Girl Weekend was birthed! With very minimal advertising, seventy women showed up on a Saturday morning for an all-day workshop at the DoubleTree hotel in Lexington, Kentucky. I did not know most of the women. They came from surrounding areas in Central Kentucky, but together we worked through the curriculum God had given me. The ladies were encouraged to pursue their God-given dreams, and as we moved through the program we stopped intermittently so that each attendee could receive one-on-one prayer. The presence of the Holy Spirit permeated and overwhelmed the workshop, and after it was over I was both hyped and exhausted at the same time. In Jeremiah 20:9, the prophet talks about "fire being shut up in [his] bones" and becoming weary because he has to get the Word of God out of him. That's how I felt as I was creating and preparing the workshop and delivering the message. I just had to let out what the LORD had placed in me. At the end of the day I told God I felt I'd done what He'd wanted me to do.

Almost immediately women started asking me when I would do another workshop. I didn't have an answer but everything within me wanted to say, "I want to do these Dream Workshops all the time, because there are tons of women who need to be encouraged to dream, and to dream big. So big, in fact, that it takes God to help them accomplish the dream." But because I was working full-time at the hospital, I couldn't commit to doing any more workshops for a while. But the thought never left me. So as I returned to my daily routine, I told any woman who would listen about that Dream Workshop, and they almost always responded by saying, "next time you do one, please let me know." Over the next few years, I often spoke with my husband about doing the Dream Workshops full-time, but I never moved forward to actually make it happen.

In January 2014, I took a position in Savannah, Georgia, as a vice-president in a teaching hospital with a Level 1 trauma center, another busy job that did not lend itself to me also running the Women's Empowerment Workshop. I continued to share what happened at that first workshop, and I even had extra copies of the original brochure.

In November 2014, I traveled to Atlanta for a nursing event and I had lunch with attorney Denise Brown-Henderson. I shared my dream with her of doing the Women's Empowerment Workshop/Dream Girl Weekend full-time. After I outlined the six workshop sessions, she quickly and excitedly said, "We need to take this on the road! I want you to do this workshop for the women at my church!" I told her I would be glad to.

At Denise's recommendation, Kenya Baldwin, who oversaw the Women's Ministry at Christians for Change Baptist Church, gave me the green light. So on September 19, 2015, I did my second Women's Empowerment Workshop/Dream Girl Weekend at the Wyndham hotel in Peachtree City, Georgia. It was a great meeting and many of the women were inspired to step out in faith and pursue their God-given dreams.

While I was focusing on developing and giving the workshop, God was also busy working on something else. In the spring of 2014, I was given a prophetic word from Pastor Verdise Bradford. She said, "God wants you to write your book. It's time." She had no idea I wanted to take the six sessions and put them into a book. I later told her that her word was confirmation because two days prior to our talk, I'd told my husband Steve that I needed to get started writing my book and had already written the first page. Since receiving that word from Pastor Bradford, I've received two more messages about writing from Bishop Leonard Gibbs and Prophet Patricia Dwight.

This book has been in the making for the past eight years in some form or another. The six sessions from the original Women's Empowerment Workshop are discussed here. The sessions include:

Dream Killers, The Dream Girl, The Dream Giver, The Dream, Write the Vision/Dream and Create a Dream Girl Network. I'm no longer working as a nurse executive in Savannah and have been using some of my time to push out this book.

My husband Steve Allison has been very supportive of me pursuing my big dream. I'm also blessed to have so many friends and family who've also said, "I believe in you, you can do this." As we pursue our dreams and achieve a measure of success, fear still pops up and has a tendency to settle in until one of our prayer partners reminds us of Isaiah 54:17, NKJV, "No weapon formed against you shall prosper." And then we're fired up again and encouraged to move forward in confidence.

I currently have a group of women who are die-hard prayer warriors, who pray on a teleconference every Monday night at 9:00 pm EST. These women are from all over the country and many have never met each other...I am the only one who knows all the women... but they know each other by the Spirit. These wonderful women pray and expect the impossible while encouraging me and one another weekly.

This book was a labor of love. My prayer is that everyone who reads it will discover and pursue their God-given dreams and walk into the destiny God planned for them before the world began. Like the women I pray with every week, you must pray and expect the impossible!

Penne Allison

CHAPTER 1

DREAM KILLERS

When was the last time you truly dreamed? When was the last time you dreamed as you used to dream when you were a little girl? When we were kids, we easily believed anything was possible. We wanted to be an architect. Check. We wanted to be an actress. Check. We wanted to be a doctor, a lawyer, a business person, an anchorwoman. Check, check, check!

But as some of us grew older, those dreams seemed to fade into the distance, and as we busied ourselves with the things of adulthood we gradually stopped dreaming actively. And then somewhere along the line, many of us may have stopped dreaming or daydreaming completely. We no longer shared our hopes and dreams with our best friends, sisters, moms, aunts, cousins, relatives and teachers. Some of us didn't even allow ourselves permission to dream when we were alone. In our minds, we didn't dare dream because the world constantly reminded us that we were too old, too poor, too busy, too young, too inexperienced or too this or too that to pursue and realize the dreams in our hearts.

But now, I invite you to dream again, and not according to the worldly dreams you may have harbored when you were a child. I encourage you to get close to God, hear His voice and discover the best dreams of all, the dreams that our loving Father God created for you before you were even born!

In *I'm a Dream Girl: A Guide to Fulfilling Your God-Given Dreams*, I want to take you on a journey upward and inward and into a sacred relationship with God, Jesus and the Holy Spirit. I want you to discover your true identity, not as a mother, wife, nurse, businessperson, etc., but your true identity as a daughter of the Most High God, as accepted, beloved, chosen, powerful and made of incorruptible seed. I want you to know exactly who you are, so that God, the Giver of Dreams, will reveal to you His precious plans for you and your life—but not so that you may be glorified—but that He may be glorified through the work that He is calling you to do. And He who created us knows us so very well that He has given us the desires of our hearts—so that what He is calling you to do will resonate with you, delight you and allow you to delight in Him in the highest way possible. That thing that you love to do, or loved to do when you were younger, that thing that is easy for you or comes naturally, the thing that gives you joy...perhaps that's where God is leading you... Come with me, and dream!

The Bible says in John 10:10, NLT, "The thief's purpose is to steal and kill and destroy. My purpose is to give them a rich and satisfying life." Christ came so that we could walk in our purpose, realize our dreams and live life to the fullest. The enemy of our souls is on his job 24/7. His primary purpose is to steal, kill and destroy every dream, vision, idea, purpose and calling he can. He is the chief dream killer and usually nearby when a dream dies and falls to the ground. But we can't blame the devil for every broken dream because sometimes we derail our own dreams by the choices we make and lifestyles we choose.

Many of us have always had a dream deep down in our hearts, but every time we try to pursue our dream, something trips us up. Something always gets in the way and hinders our progress. For many of us, fulfilling our dreams has become a distant fantasy we believe we cannot reach; things crop up and ruin our chances of success. We find ourselves saying, "I guess it wasn't meant to be," or "Life just happens!" Sometimes it is not just one thing that blocks our dreams, but many things. Things that prevent us from fulfilling our dreams are what I call "Dream Killers." These saboteurs appear in many different ways. In this chapter we will unpack some of the dream killers and strategies to overcome them.

Negative Words

"The tongue has the power of life and death, and those who love it will eat its fruit." (Proverbs 18:21, NIV) "And the tongue is a flame of fire. It is a whole world of wickedness, corrupting your entire body. It can set your whole life on fire, for it is set on fire by hell itself. People can tame all kinds of animals, birds, reptiles, and fish, but no one can tame the tongue. It is restless and evil, full of deadly poison. Sometimes it praises our Lord and Father, and sometimes it curses those who have been made in the image of God. And so blessing and cursing come pouring out of the same mouth. Surely, my brothers and sisters, this is not right!" (James, 3:6-10. NLT).

The words we speak are very important because words contain the power of life and death. So we have to be careful of how we use our tongue because the tongue is a powerful force and difficult to control. The tongue can speak blessings and curses. When we take control over what comes out of our mouths, we will change the quality of our lives. The words we attach to our lives become part of our lives. When we carelessly speak ill of ourselves and our dreams, we are framing our future. The Bible says in Hebrews 11:3 KJV, "Through faith we understand that the worlds were framed by the word of God, so that things which are seen were not made of things which do appear." Just as God framed the world with His word, we too frame our world with our words. We must be intentional about speaking life over every dream seed God has placed inside of us. Every vision, calling and purpose must be pushed out with positive words, not negative ones. A sense of hope must accompany every breath we speak over our lives. Negative words can kill our dreams, so we must always speak life.

Unbelief

When God places within us a dream or vision that's big, we often cannot believe He would use *us* in such a magnificent way. We find ourselves not believing our dream can happen, and dwelling in unbelief is a dangerous place to be. The Children of Israel left Egypt seeing and experiencing one of the biggest wonders ever recorded. They walked across the Red Sea on dry ground while Pharaoh's army drowned behind them. The Children of Israel were led by a cloud by day and pillar of fire by night, and were given fresh manna every morning. A trip that should have taken about eleven days by foot ended up taking forty years! They kept going around the same mountain grumbling and complaining and not believing God. He allowed them to wander in the wilderness until a whole generation died off. He did not let the people who came out of Egypt enter the Promised Land because of their unbelief. After all of the signs, wonders and miracles God performed for them while they were in the wilderness, they still did not believe. "The people refused to enter the pleasant land, for they wouldn't believe his promise to care for them." (Psalms 106:24, NLT)

In Numbers 13, Moses sent twelve spies into Canaan to explore the Promised Land. Ten came back and said they couldn't take the land because its people were bigger than they were. But two spies, Caleb and Joshua, said they were well able to conquer the "giants" and take control of the land. Yet and still, the Israelites believed the majority report of the ten rather than the minority report of Caleb and Joshua.

God wants us to believe *Him* even if He told just one person to do great and mighty exploits, and even if the majority of people around his messenger don't believe. When God says move, we must move. When He says stand still, we must stand still. Unbelief keeps us inactive and in a mode of distrust. Hebrews 4:6, KJV, says, "Seeing therefore it remaineth that some must enter therein, and they to whom it was first preached entered not in because of unbelief." If we don't believe God, if we don't do what He tells us to do because we don't believe, we are disobeying Him. Unbelief in this instance is the same as disobedience. We must not allow unbelief to keep us from moving forward into the destiny God has for us.

Procrastination

"A nap here, a nap there, a day off here, a day off there, sit back, take it easy—do you know what comes next? Just this: You can look forward to a dirt-poor life, with poverty as your permanent houseguest!" (Proverbs 24:33-34, MSG). "Do not boast about tomorrow, for you do not know what a day may bring." (Proverbs 27:1, NIV). "Lazy people want much but get little, but those who work hard will prosper." (Proverbs 13:4, NLT).

When we constantly put things off until a later date, we eventually lose out on what's in store for us. For some, the dreams God has placed inside of us may become our livelihood. But when we don't work hard toward making that dream a reality, we end up at the bottom rather than on top where God intended us to be. If we can accomplish something today toward the dreams and visions God has given us, then we should do it now and not wait until tomorrow. We never know what tomorrow will bring. We must trust and believe that whatever we, the children of God, put our hands to will prosper. When we lay back, waste time and procrastinate, we should not expect things to get accomplished. Where there's a will there's a way. When people give excuses as to why they haven't made significant progress toward achieving their dream, sometimes it's simply laziness. Those who want much will get very little if they are lazy. God is looking to accomplish great things through the diligent. "He who has a slack hand becomes poor, But the hand of the diligent makes rich." (Proverbs 10:4, NKJV) Sometimes procrastination is not laziness but rather a habit to wait until the last minute, and that may be because we have too many things on our plate. But when we seek God first and His righteousness (Matthew 6:33), He will show us what needs to be on our plate and what needs to come off. Even if it is not related to laziness, procrastination is a habit that greatly affects our destiny. In some instances, procrastination is linked to fear. We wait to get started because of fear of failure or fear of success. Many times we procrastinate because we don't want to appear inadequate, ineffective or incompetent.

Procrastination is a major dream killer.

Fear

Fear is most likely the number one dream killer and is the root of many of our challenges. It sometimes paralyzes us and renders us inactive. 2 Timothy 1:7, NKJV, says, "For God has not given us a spirit of fear, but of power and of love and of a sound mind." So we must remember if we're fearful, fear is not from God. Satan uses scare tactics to keep us bound by fear. The Bible says that the devil walks about like a roaring lion seeking whom he will devour (I Peter 5:8), but God calls us to be alert, courageous and confident, and willing to go after the hard or difficult situations in our lives. He will fight our battles for us; all we need to do is stand up and fight and confront the enemy. God has already promised us victory through the saving power of Jesus.

Sometimes we fear failure or success, or we fear what people may think or say about us, but each time we face fear and win, we become more confident for the next battle or moment of intimidation. Being courageous and strong is not a suggestion of God's, but a commandment. In Joshua 1:9, NKJV, God encouraged Joshua and the children of Israel, saying, "Have I not commanded you? Be strong and of good courage; do not be afraid, nor be dismayed, for the LORD your God *is* with you wherever you go." And earlier, in Joshua 1:6 and 1:7, God also tells them to be strong and courageous. So don't be scared. Do not allow the enemy to intimidate you. Our precious Father God is with you wherever you go. So, as you pursue your dream, when you're afraid, don't run and hide. Be strong and courageous and keep moving. Just do the next thing that God is calling you to do. Nothing is more important than following hard and fast what God says to do. And as we obey Him and follow Him, we will reap a harvest.

Victim Thinking/Mentality

According to the Merriam-Webster Learner's Dictionary a victim mentality is, " : the belief that you are always a victim : the idea that bad things always happen to you." An example of victim thinking is found in the Bible in John 5. A disabled man sat by a pool for thirty-eight years hoping to get well. That's an awfully long time to wait to get healed. In John 5:5-8, NIV, the text states: "When Jesus saw him lying there and learned that he had been in this condition for a long time, he asked him, 'Do you want to get well?' 'Sir,' the invalid replied, 'I have no one to help me into the pool when the water is stirred. While I am trying to get in, someone else goes down ahead of me.' Then Jesus said to him, 'Get up! Pick up your mat and walk.'"

The man had been sitting by the pool for such a long time he could not even fathom being next to be healed. Even when Jesus asked him if he wanted to be healed, he did not say "yes" right away, but launched into a story about how he had been a victim year after year of not being the first to get in the pool. Then Jesus said simply that the man should pick up his bed and walk.

Can you imagine being healed by Jesus after being sick for thirty-eight years? Victim thinking makes us forget our dreams and makes us feel powerless. A victim mentality keeps us bound, broken and stuck. When we see ourselves as a victim, our brokenness is always someone else's fault. "I have no one to help me into the pool," as the man comments in John 5:7, is a statement that places blame on others. Being stuck mentally thus becomes a way of life. When we stay in victim mode, other people are at fault as to why we are in a particular predicament, and this leads us to abdicate responsibility for our healing and our lives. We don't have to risk failing.

Being a victim is neither right nor wrong, it's just a choice we make. We may slip into victim thinking, but we must not dwell there. Every day we get to choose whether to focus on the difficulties and problems in our lives or focus on ways to find solutions and move toward our dreams. If being a victim works for us and we get the results we want, then we can remain a victim. But I would venture to say that being a victim does not work, nor does it produce the desired outcomes necessary to fulfill our destiny. Victim thinking kills any dream we might have.

Next time we cry out and say, "I just can't win for losing," and want to invite our friends to a pity party, think about making a different choice. When we become aware of our own whining and complaining, we can choose differently. Over and over and again we must choose not to be a victim, for it's not a onetime choice. In every situation in our lives, we can instead choose to be a victor.

We'll never achieve our dreams as long as we play the victim role. Jesus commanded the man by the pool to pick up his bed and walk, so get up! Take up your bed, aka your problems, and get on with your life! Victim thinking is a definite dream killer.

Unhealthy Relationships

There are so many types of unhealthy relationships in the world that I cannot begin to name them all here. But we'll deal with a few because many times our relationships drive and affect everything else in our lives—even the dreams God has placed within our hearts and minds. When close relationships fall apart, the process takes a toll on us, sometimes rendering us unable to move forward. Many times unhealthy relationships push us to the brink of breakdown and, at times, the point of no return. Relationships are powerful because a part of our soul is wrapped up in the other person so much that any break may cause a tear so deep it wounds our very souls.

There's an old saying: "When Mama is not happy, nobody is happy." When a woman is in a relationship and she becomes fractured, her state affects the entire household. The woman in many instances is seen as the heart of the home. If the heart is broken, then the rest of the household feels the pain. When a woman is broken from relationship issues, dreams become deferred, deflated and stagnant, and then they die. There is nothing more painful than seeing a vibrant woman full of dreams, visions and ambition fall by the wayside into a place of nothingness. Some unhealthy relationships are abusive, domineering, passive, passive-aggressive, maternalistic, paternalistic, people pleasing, unequally yoked, co-dependent and much more.

When women are in unhealthy relationships, they may respond by using a variety of coping mechanisms. Many are co-dependent and want someone to do something for them. Their self-esteem and self-image are compromised and their dreams get put on the shelf.

For various reasons, they cover habitually for those they love or those they tolerate and remain connected to. Some women move into attention-seeking mode and behave in a way that silently asks, "Will someone please notice me?" Others have an approval addiction and want to know, "Will someone please like me?" Yet other women have validation issues and need to know, "Will someone please tell me I am important?" Some women are control freaks and wonder, "Will I ever trust someone to take care of me?" But when we seek attention, approval, validation and control, we get wrapped up in unhealthy relationships and lose our focus. The relationship trumps everything and our dreams fall by the wayside. Even when our relationships are intact and healthy, we must be properly aligned with those around us as we move forward with our dreams. When we change, everyone around us will be forced to change. Sometimes people in our relationship sphere don't want to change and in some instances refuse to change. When we get ready to pursue our dreams, some people will say to us "I don't think this is the right time," or "I'm not sure if you have enough resources," and give a host of other reasons why you shouldn't move forward—but fear is usually the reason. Some folks will try to make us fearful when we announce that we're starting to pursue our dreams. Some people will tell us that we should just maintain the status quo, that there's no need to change. We should just leave things as they are. These are the folks in our lives who are mortified by change.

Other people will point out how many problems you'll run into and try to convince you that whatever you're pursuing just isn't possible, that it can't or won't be done. Their mantra is, "It's impossible!" Then worst of all is the person in your life who declares, "Over my dead body! I'm not going to let you do it!" People who hold that opinion actually try to block your efforts with threats and intimidation.

Struggling with unhealthy relationships is probably the number one reason people just give up and quit pursuing their dreams. Working on creating and maintaining healthy relationships will help move the dream along, but we must get help from God. He placed dreams deep inside us, and as we work to activate those dreams, we must ask God to work on the relationships in our lives. Support for our dreams is a must. Without support there will be constant conflict because usually the dreams God places in our hearts are huge.

The Bible is full of intriguing relationship drama. In Genesis 37, there's a story about Joseph, the favorite son of Jacob. In Genesis 37:5-11, Joseph received two dreams which indicated he would one day become a person of authority and stature greater than anyone in his family. This was a huge God-sized dream! Joseph would in fact one day reign over many people, including his family, but when Joseph initially shared his dream with his relatives, his siblings hated him and his father scolded him. His brothers rejected him and his dream and they plotted to kill him, but ended up selling him into slavery. According to Genesis 37:18-19, NLT, "When Joseph's brothers saw him coming, they recognized him in the distance. As he approached, they made plans to kill him. 'Here comes the dreamer!' they said.'" They mocked him because he was a dreamer. Sharing the dream sparked unhealthy behavior from his siblings.

Even though he became an Egyptian slave, Joseph knew his destiny was much greater. As the story in Genesis 37-50 reveals, Joseph wound up in a pit, Potiphar's house, prison and finally the palace, but we can learn many lessons from Joseph's life: 1) We can't tell our dreams to everybody, not even people who are supposed to be close to us; 2) Know with assurance that when the dream is from God, it will come to pass, so stay in faith and remain hopeful; 3) Process stands between the promise of a dream and the fulfillment of a dream; 4) As you are going through the process of making your dream a reality, stay true to God and maintain good character. God will show favor even in difficult situations.

David and Bathsheba are another example of an unhealthy relationship in the Bible. Bathsheba was a married woman who King David took for himself. According to 2 Samuel 11:2-3, NIV, "One evening David got up from his bed and walked around on the roof of the palace. From the roof he saw a woman bathing. The woman was very beautiful, and David sent someone to find out about her. The man said, 'She is Bathsheba, the daughter of Eliam and the wife of Uriah the Hittite.'" Then David sent messengers to get her. She came to him. And he had sex with her. Then she went back home. All of that took place after she had already made herself "clean" from her monthly period. Later, Bathsheba found out she was pregnant, and she sent a message to David. This illicit relationship took David off course and he ended up having Bathsheba's husband killed on the frontline of battle. The child born to this union died as a baby.

Any immoral relationships will create unnecessary situations in our lives that we will have to deal with. But while we're dealing with unnecessary situations, we're wasting time not pursuing the dreams God has for us.

Busyness and Living Other People's Dreams

The world has become so busy it's frightening. It seems that we are connected to our devices 24/7. Being too busy keeps us out of balance, and having too many "irons in the fire" and not focusing on what's most important derails our dreams. Being tired all the time is not God's best for us. If we are tired all the time, we must reevaluate our schedule. Every person has the same amount of time every day: twenty-four hours. Our productivity is determined by how we prioritize our twenty-four hours. It may not seem like it, but we do have control of our schedule. We must learn when and how to say "yes" to some things and "no" to others.

Some of the biggest time wasters are television, the internet and social media. According to A.C. Nielsen Company, the average American watches more than four hours of T.V. each day. Imagine if we spent four hours a day hearing from God and pursuing our God-given dreams? The world would never be the same!

Social media and reality TV are outlets that allow us to peer into other lives. We see snapshots of what people want us to see and then we begin to long for what's happening in their world. So we busy ourselves by watching reality shows or constantly checking Facebook, Instagram and Snapchat to see how others are living. Instead of pursuing the dream God gave us, we live vicariously through others.

Our culture is obsessed with reality shows; we like drama and plenty of it, every day. I wonder sometimes if the reason we are so interested in other people's lives is because we have not found our purpose. But the truth is that we'll never find our purpose or our true identity, or realize God's dreams for us by losing ourselves in mounds and mounds of television and social media. Hollywood and TV are fantasy, not reality. When we get a revelation of our own purpose, we will quickly realize we've been wasting precious time trying to be like so-and-so. We must be the best version of ourselves and go after the dreams and the purpose God created just for us.

The best recommendation I will give in this book is…TURN OFF THE TELEVISION, GET OFF FACEBOOK and FACE THE GOOD BOOK! The good book is the Bible, the infallible Word of God, and it is always relevant. If you are addicted to television and social media, periodically take time to rest and fast from the screen. Instead of catching up on your favorite show or checking Twitter, daily spend time seeking God in connection to your own life. Write down what God says as He reveals His plan for you.

Since the average person spends four hours a day on television, maybe start with giving God thirty minutes a day and increase from there until you devote more time to Him than you give to watching a screen.

Our constant scurrying around in circles accomplishing very little is a dream killer. Don't be deceived—busyness is the oldest trick the enemy of our soul uses to derail God's best plan for us. God wants us to be totally sold out to Him and a Disciple of Christ for life. As stated in Luke 14:33, NKJV, "So likewise, whoever of you does not forsake all that he has cannot be My disciple."

Illness and Injury

I have spent over thirty years working in hospitals as a nurse, mostly in emergency services. I've seen hundreds of patients in and out of emergency departments looking for healing. Illnesses and injuries come in many shapes and sizes, and can be acute or chronic. No matter the problem the answer is always found in healing and wholeness. There have been times when patients come in and have been so sick that no one expected them to live. But then miraculously, they walk out of the hospital days later. As a medical professional, I've been taught the scientific method and believe there is a place for modern medical treatment; however, I also believe in divine healing. Some of the cases I have seen can only be explained as miracles.

When Jesus was getting ready to go back to heaven after the resurrection, He spoke to His disciples about what they were to do on earth after He left. Most believers embrace the Great Commission found in Matthew 28:18-19 NLT: Jesus came and told His disciples, "I have been given all authority in heaven and on earth. Therefore, go and make disciples of all the nations, baptizing them in the name of the Father and the Son and the Holy Spirit. Teach these disciples to obey all the commands I have given you, and be sure of this: I am with you always, even to the end of the age." The disciples could not carry out the Great Commission in their own strength and authority, but they would be able to do it in the authority of Jesus Christ. Jesus sent the Holy Spirit to be with them to help them accomplish what needed to be done.

Mark also records this account of Jesus going back to heaven, but his words included some other things as well. Mark 16:15-18 NLT, Then He told them, "Go into all the world and preach the Good News to everyone. Anyone who believes and is baptized will be saved. But anyone who refuses to believe will be condemned. These miraculous signs will accompany those who believe. They will cast out demons in my name; and they will speak in new languages, they will be able to handle snakes with safety, and if they drink anything poisonous it won't hurt them. They will be able to place their hands on the sick, and they will be healed." The last words of Jesus before He ascended give us insight into what He thought was important. Among those things was healing. I believe He wants us to experience healing even on this side of heaven. It is in the name of the Lord, in His strength not our own. Jesus worked through the disciples and He works through us today. Mark 16:20 says, "And the disciples went everywhere and preached, and the Lord worked through them, confirming what they said by many miraculous signs."

Some people believe God is punishing them with sickness because of their sins. John 10:10 NLT says, The thief's purpose is to steal, kill and destroy. My purpose is to give them a rich and satisfying life. Jesus came so that we might have life, a full satisfying life." Sickness and disease sometimes hinder us from walking out our purpose as God had planned for us. Just as Jesus has purpose, the enemy of our soul has a purpose too, to steal, kill and destroy.

All illness and disease we encounter is not from the enemy. Some of our illnesses come from stress and a lack of self-care. We must take responsibility for many of our health issues. We must get proper nutrition, rest, exercise, recreation and stress relief. And if we're honest with ourselves, we don't always do these things. Many of us want a miracle—we want to be "healed," when all we really need is to get up and go to the gym and stop eating unhealthy foods. Sometimes we don't need a miracle, we just need to better manage our lives.

Some people have done all the right things in terms of eating healthy foods, exercising, getting rest and living a stress-free life and still end up sick. I don't profess to know all the reasons people get sick and why some get healed and some don't. I can only say what the Bible says and nothing more. Mark tells us to lay hands on the sick and they will be healed. The book of James also gives us some insight into prayer and healing for the sick. James 5:14-15 NLT says, "Are any of you sick? You should call for the elders of the church to come pray over you, anointing you with oil in the name of the Lord. Such a prayer offered in faith will heal the sick, and the Lord will make you well, and if you have committed any sins, you will be forgiven."

Sometimes we bring illness on ourselves by the lifestyle choices we make. It appears accidents and illnesses just happen to us. Nothing just happens. If we don't create an environment for sickness, then the enemy of our souls launches outright attacks to lure us into unhealthy addictions and emotional instability. When we yield to temptations and indulge in the wrong things, the enemy is happy to undermine God's best plan for us. Jesus died that we might be healed in every way. Jesus became a curse for us so we can have victory over any curse. We must acknowledge what we are in need of, ask for healing and receive our healing. We can pray for ourselves, but sometimes it is good to get in agreement with other believers and ask the leaders of the church to pray over you.

The Bible says, "He personally carried our sin in his body on the cross so that we can be dead to sin and live for what is right. By his wounds you are healed." (II Peter 2:24 NLT). Some people believe the healing here refers to spiritual healing. Jesus's completed work on the cross was for total wholeness, including physical healing. Many times the Dream Killers called illness and injury keep us from moving forward.

Negative Strongholds

I saved negative strongholds for last because it is by far the biggest category that keeps us hindered, bound and at a standstill when it comes to our dreams. Before we talk about individual strongholds, I want to describe what strongholds are and how they work while highlighting the key scripture that discusses how to destroy such negative entities in our lives. People in church circles talk about strongholds a lot but rarely give specifics on how to demolish them.

What is a stronghold? In Biblical times, a stronghold was a fortified brick wall that cities ran to during a time of war. A stronghold was where the army could retreat and find safety in a very strong fortress, a place from which they could defend themselves. The Greek word for stronghold is *ochuroma*, which means to fortify by holding safely. In a biblical context, a stronghold is what a person uses to fortify or defend a personal belief, idea and opinion against outside opposition. The key passage we want to examine is 2 Corinthians 10:3-5, NLT, which says: "We are human, but we don't wage war as humans do. We use God's mighty weapons, not worldly weapons, to knock down strongholds of human reasoning and to destroy false arguments. We destroy every proud obstacle that keeps people from knowing God. We capture their rebellious thoughts and teach them to obey Christ."

Our minds are the place in which strongholds are erected. Ideas, opinions, beliefs, human reasoning and false arguments all start in the mind. Some of our opinions, ideas and beliefs come from experiences we have had in our lives, whether good or bad. Some ideas are planted by the enemy himself. Our mind is the battleground for Satan, the enemy of our souls. The enemy is very cunning. He feeds our minds lies and deceives us on a regular basis.

A negative stronghold could develop from something traumatic that happened in our lives as children. For example, when you were a little girl, your family fell on hard times and there was not enough food in the house. Many nights you went to bed hungry. Then your father left the family and things got worse, and your family was put out in the streets and had to sleep in an abandoned warehouse. Your mom told you that God was punishing the family because of some wrongdoings she had committed years ago. As a child you begin to form opinions and ideas about the so-called God. Maybe your opinion was one of being rejected and unloved by Him. You continue with this mindset throughout your life and other things happen that reinforce your beliefs about an unloving God who constantly rejects you. Once you reach adulthood, a negative stronghold has not only been erected but also fortified. At this point, you can take on anyone and defend your position based on your belief. Negative strongholds are almost always a way to keep us from knowing God. In reality, He is a loving God who accepts us and wants the best for us. After many years of fortifying a negative stronghold and defending our position, destroying such a stronghold can be a challenge. Negative strongholds come about from human reasoning and false arguments that we rehearse over and over in our minds. To demolish destructive strongholds, we must use Godly weapons.

The first weapon to begin the demolition is truth. The truth of God's word can knock down negative strongholds. When we believe and defend a lie, the solution is always truth. If we feel unloved, we must get some words straight from the throne of God that say: "Yes, I have loved you with an everlasting love; therefore with lovingkindness I have drawn you." (Jeremiah 31:3, NKJV) "For God so loved the world that He gave His only begotten Son, that whoever believes in Him should not perish but have everlasting life." (John 3:16, NKJV) "For He Himself has said, 'I will never leave you nor forsake you.'" (Hebrews 13:5, NKJV)

When we renew our minds with the Word of God, He will transform the way we think, thus transforming the way we behave. Negative strongholds keep us bound. The enemy knows if he keeps the strongholds erected and we continue to defend them, we don't have any chance of realizing our God-given dreams, visions, calling and purpose. Jesus had to deal with the enemy coming after him in the wilderness during his fast. He tried to tempt Jesus three times. Each time the enemy came forth with lies, Jesus brought the truth by speaking the Word of God. There is power in speaking the Word into the atmosphere. The Word of God has power, whether Jesus speaks it or whether we speak it: "For the word of God is living and powerful, and sharper than any two-edged sword, piercing even to the division of soul and spirit, and of the joints and marrow, and is a discerner of the thought and intents of the heart." (Hebrews 4:12, NKJV) The Word of God is also known as the Sword of the Spirit in Ephesians 6. Use the Word of God as an offensive weapon to tear down destructive strongholds.

Another Godly weapon we can use is prayer. Prayer is simply talking to God about the strongholds and releasing them to Him. Holding on to some of the strongholds is quite simply holding on to lies and defending lies, and this is sin. The Bible says, "If we confess our sins, He is faithful and just to forgive us *our* sins and to cleanse us from all unrighteousness." (1 John 1:9, NKJV) Use prayer time to praise and thank God, confess known and unknown sins and ask Him to tear down the negative strongholds in our lives. Just like speaking the word daily, prayer is a weapon we must use daily too. Pray in the spirit as the Holy Spirit gives you utterance.

Fasting is another weapon. When a negative stronghold is fortified over time, you may want to consider a fast. Fasting is abstaining from food for a spiritual purpose—it's not a diet. Fasting is done to quiet our flesh— to subdue our wants, needs and desires so that we can better hear from God. When we declutter our lives by abstaining from food for a certain amount of time, we are able to go deeper with God into a place of intimacy and sensitivity. There, God can communicate with us with clarity and power and show us the root of what is hindering us, or He can reveal things to us that we may be otherwise too distracted to understand or see.

There are different types of fasts. You should ask God what type is best for you when seeking delivery from negative strongholds. Fasting may include refraining from a meal or two a day, or it could be to refrain from all food for a day or longer. It could be refraining from snacks, or, for those who have medical problems and cannot go without food, it may be refraining from sugar, chocolate, etc.

If you feel that God is leading you to fast about a certain situation in your life, pray and ask for direction. If you have never fasted, or have health issues, it's best to consult a medical and spiritual professional before you start your fast. If you are unable to fast for medical reasons, you may consider doing a TV or social media fast. When you fast, the idea is to step away for a time, from anything that is hindering you from hearing from the LORD.

Fasting takes our focus off the physical and puts it on the spiritual. Our hunger is directed toward God and hearing Him. Fasting is not just so God can do something for us, but it is to transform us by His Spirit to live in total dependence on Him and not rely on ourselves. When we are desperate to live on purpose, it may take a season of fasting to accomplish all God has for us. Jentezen Franklin says in *Fasting*, his 2008 book, "Fasting puts you in the mainstream of God's priorities."

Another Godly weapon is praise, which has a way of cutting through the atmosphere and changing it for God's glory. In the Old Testament, there's a famous story in 2 Chronicles about King Jehoshaphat in which God uses praise as the weapon to slay an army. If God can do that, He can surely use our praise to bring down the negative strongholds in our lives.

King Jehoshaphat got the word that there were several armies coming to attack him and his people. Needless to say Jehoshaphat was terrified. He was so afraid in fact that he called for a fast for himself and his people. When Jehoshaphat gathered the people together, he began to pray to God. He reminded God of how mighty He was and the covenant God made with Jehoshaphat's ancestor Abraham. He even reminded God that Abraham was His friend! Jehoshaphat uttered this prayer right in front of the temple where God's name was honored, and He led the people in crying out to God and asking Him to save and rescue them. He admitted how powerless he and his people were against the armies that were on the way. He confessed that they did not know what to do. Just as Jehoshaphat was leading the people in prayer, God's Spirit came upon the prophet Jahaziel. who said as the Lord's messenger, "Do not be afraid! Don't be discouraged by this mighty army, for the battle is not yours, but God's." (2 Chronicles 20:15, NLT)

Through Jahaziel, God gave King Jehoshaphat and his men the exact battle plan. They were to go out on the next day and they would not need to fight. God's desire was that they just take their positions on the battlefield, stand still and watch the Lord's victory. God would be with them. So they did as the Lord had instructed. King Jehoshaphat appointed singers to walk ahead of the army, singing and praising the Lord. They sang: "Give thanks to the LORD; his faithful love endures forever!" (2 Chronicles 20:21, NLT) When they were in place and began to sing, the armies that came out against them began to kill themselves. When Jehoshaphat and his men went to the overlook, all they saw were dead bodies. God had set ambushes and fought the battle for the Israelites that day. Praise is a great weapon! Jehoshaphat praised and thanked the Lord for the victory in the Valley of Blessing.

King Jehoshaphat used three weapons—fasting, prayer and praise. Negative stronghold battles will not be won in the flesh or by trying to be good; they only will be won when we fast, pray and give God praise. Pulling down strongholds will not be done with carnal weapons, only spiritual ones. Take control and reign over your busy life. Get before the God of Glory in humble submission and pray, fast and praise. You will be amazed how He answers. As 2 Corinthians 10:4-5, NKJV, states: "For the weapons of our warfare are not carnal but mighty in God for pulling down strongholds, casting down arguments and every high thing that exalts itself against the knowledge of God, bringing every thought into captivity to the obedience of Christ…"

Now let's examine a few of the strongholds that we most often deal with. This is not an exhaustive list of destructive strongholds, but rather enough to give us a starting point. We will look at unforgiveness, guilt, shame, condemnation, rejection and sexual immorality.

Unforgiveness

When we have been hurt deeply. the most immediate protective mechanism is to put up a wall and not allow in anyone who could repeat the offense. We set up the stronghold then defend our positions with sentiments like, "This person does not deserve forgiveness." "I will never forgive this person." "I can't forgive, I just can't." "I am deeply hurt and I will not forgive." Refusing to forgive is like drinking poison and expecting the other person to die.

Unforgiveness is toxic and it creates many problems for us. Some people think, "If I forgive the person who's harmed me, I'll appear weak. So I refuse to let anyone walk all over me." Others reason: "I will withhold forgiveness to make the person pay dearly for hurting me." Sometimes the scars go so deep, and forgiving the person never crosses our minds. Unforgiveness keeps us stuck in the place of our pain. How tragic it is to be wounded and wallow in our wounds, remembering every day of our lives the person who inflicted the pain.

If left unaddressed, unforgiveness may eventually lead to feelings of bitterness, anger, resentment, pride and many other negative emotions. If we don't learn to forgive, our hearts will harden over time. Years will go by and people around us will wonder what happened to us and try to figure out why we're so angry. Unforgiveness will be at the root of the problem. Even if we are unable to forgive just one person, that could block us from realizing all that God has for us. Unless we truly let go of the offense, we'll never walk in our true purpose and the freedom of our dreams. It's said that high blood pressure is the silent killer, but unforgiveness is the real silent killer; it's an inside job and it's insidious. Unforgiveness is now considered a disease in some medical books, and Dr. Michael Barry states in his publication *The Forgiveness Project,* that 61 percent of cancer patients have an issue with forgiveness.

Ephesians 4:32, NIV, encourages us to, "Be kind and compassionate to one another, forgiving each other, just as in Christ God forgave you." Jesus told Peter that he should forgive his brother not seven times, but "seventy times seven." (Matthew 18:22, NLV) If you're having a problem forgiving someone—or yourself!—prayer is always a good place to start. Pray for the one who has harmed you, and by faith, release them to God. We can't forgive in our own strength, but with God all things are possible, even forgiveness. Deciding to let someone (or yourself) off the hook will be one of the best days of your life. Don't delay.

Truth demolishes negative strongholds. The truth about forgiveness is that Jesus taught us to forgive and expects us to forgive. As seen in Matthew 6:12, 14-15, NKJV, he states: "And forgive us our debts, As we forgive our debtors. ... For if you forgive men their trespasses, your heavenly Father will also forgive you. But if you do not forgive men their trespasses, neither will your Father forgive your trespasses."

Forgiveness is a big deal. Unforgiveness can single-handedly kill any dream. Forgive and be free.

Guilt, Shame and Condemnation

Guilt, shame and condemnation…these three terms go together. Guilt is about what we've done; shame is about who we are and how we see ourselves; and condemnation is about the strong accusatory voice of blame and disapproval. Many times guilt, shame and condemnation are used interchangeably, but they're distinct words, all designed to make us feel badly about ourselves or something we did.

One definition of guilt is, "1 : the fact of having committed a breach of conduct especially violating the law and involving a penalty; broadly: guilty conduct. 2 a : the state of one who has committed an offense especially consciously." (merriam-webster.com) The definition of guilt also includes "feelings of culpability especially for imagined offenses or from a sense of inadequacy." Basically, guilt is how we feel over what we've done wrong.

Shame is defined, among other things, as "a painful emotion caused by consciousness of guilt, shortcoming, or impropriety." (merriam-webster.com) Shame is how we see ourselves or feel about ourselves because of the things we've done, or we can feel shame because of things that happened to us, such as abuse or violation.

Shame usually starts early in our lives when people around us say things like, "You should be ashamed of yourself!" or "Shame on you!" or "You are so shame-faced." These expressions aim to make us feel bad about something we did, carrying over into adulthood.

As adults, we learn unhealthy coping skills to deal with shame. We cover up our shame with religious activity and/or busy ourselves with trying to make up for what we feel inside. Religious activity or "works" is where we get our self-worth and self-esteem. We never want to face God with any of our shame because it further reveals our unworthiness and the fact that we have missed the mark. Shame is bad news because it keeps us going in circles and prevents us from receiving the freedom of the completed work Christ did for us on the cross. He removed our shame; He took it on Himself. Our past is over, but the enemy keeps throwing our past in our faces and piling on as much shame as he can. If we have been violated emotionally or physically, the enemy wants us to feel dirty, like damaged goods. Just as when Adam and Eve sinned, they felt ashamed and hid from God. The enemy wants to keep us hiding out and believing that people will never accept us. Damaging thoughts can arise from shame, like "If people really knew me they would not like me." Or, "If they knew what happened to me and what kind of person I grew into, they would run from me." When the stronghold of shame is erected in our minds, everything we do is filtered through that shame.

Condemnation is "a statement or expression of very strong and definite criticism or disapproval." (merriam-webster.com) Condemnation is an accusing voice from the enemy. When dealing with the strongholds of guilt, shame and condemnation, we must be careful because such strongholds are very powerful and could potentially stop us in our tracks from pursuing the dream that God has for us by making us feel unworthy and less than.

But we must remember that our past is just that, our past. Once we accept what Christ has done—freed us from all guilt, shame and condemnation—and we accept that His blood covers our mistakes, we can live freely. As we come to understand this, we will abide in the fact that Jesus came to free us from shame.

Condemnation is from the enemy. God never condemns us. The Holy Spirit convicts us, which is very different from condemnation. The Holy Spirit invites us to turn from our wrong and repent, and then seek forgiveness and reconciliation from the Father. Remember, to begin to knock down the strongholds of guilt, shame and condemnation, we must begin with truth. As Romans 8:1, NKJV says, "… there is no condemnation for those who are in Christ Jesus."

Rejection

Rejection is probably one of the hardest things to overcome. Every person on earth wants to have a sense of belonging and acceptance. Studies and reports have proven over and over that when children are not accepted by their family, they will look outside the family unit to find a place to belong. Many times the places they find may not be the healthiest places to belong. When children are adopted, placed in foster care, abandoned or have to move from house to house, they grow up with ideas of not being wanted. The wounds of rejection are deep, so deep they can lead to depression, self-pity, anger, insecurity and a spirit of heaviness. God made us to live in community with others, not to be isolated and alone. Rejection is a cycle. When people feel rejected, they tend to pull back and isolate themselves, which then leads to more feelings of rejection. Some people who have a spirit of rejection may not hide in their shell but do the opposite, thus appearing to be the life of the party. We may do lots of favors for people just to be accepted. We may rely on perfectionism or over-achievement and rationalize that if we can be perfect or smart, people will certainly not reject us.

Rejection can thwart the pursuit of our dreams in a myriad of ways. We can immerse ourselves in materialism as a way to try and combat rejection, believing that if we have lots of material things, people can't reject us. Or we believe that if we can have this person sexually, then we will feel better and not feel rejected. Sometimes rejection manifests as pride, and we say we are better than those who reject us. The worse kind of rejection is self-rejection. People are made to be loved and accepted, and when they are not, they rebel.

Rejection started in the garden when Adam and Eve sinned and rejected the truth of God, believing the lie of Satan. When Christ came to save the world, He was rejected. 1 Peter 2:4, NLT says, "You are coming to Christ, who is the living cornerstone of God's temple. He was rejected by people, but he was chosen by God for great honor."

The stronghold of rejection can be conquered by believing the truth of God and not accepting the lie of the enemy. God does not reject us. He openly accepts us. "To the praise of the glory of His grace, by which He made us accepted in the Beloved (Ephesians 1:6 NKJV).

Sexual Immorality

Sexuality is a gift from God and was originally intended to be shared by a man and a woman inside the covenant of marriage. But something good has been turned into many perverted things. Many lives have been torn apart by sexual sins, and these illicit acts are major strongholds that keep us from walking as God would have us walk. Fornication, adultery, infidelity, licentiousness (lacking legal or moral restraint, especially sexual restraint), lasciviousness (lewd, lustful behavior), pornography, orgies, sodomy, bisexuality, homosexuality, bestiality—all of these are destructive strongholds and involve soul ties, emotional bonds that result from sexual relations. Soul ties, when not acknowledged, addressed and dealt with (most situations require the help of a trained counselor) will keep you bound in a cycle of dangerous relationships, and that's why the Bible instructs us to steer clear of sexual immorality. 1 Corinthians 6:18-20, NLT, says, "Run from sexual sin! No other sin so clearly affects the body as this one does. For sexual immorality is a sin against your own body. Don't you realize that your body is the temple of the Holy Spirit, who lives in you and was given to you by God? You do not belong to yourself, for God bought you with a high price. So you must honor God with your body."

The negative stronghold of sexual immorality has become common place in our society and many would argue that calling it sin is old school and perhaps somewhat narrow. Women in particular love very deeply and the sexual intimacy seals the emotional tie. This is not an easy topic to discuss and must be handled as Jesus handled these discussions. In the book of John Jesus models for us how we are to respond when topics like this come up. In John 8 there was a woman caught in adultery and the religious leaders brought the woman to Jesus and said, the law of Moses says we should stone her what do you think we should do? He immediately said, "alright, but let the one who has never sinned throw the first stone!" (John 8:7b NLT). All of the woman's accusers left one by one until only the woman and Jesus remained. Jesus said to her, "Where are your accusers? Didn't even one of them condemn you?" "No Lord," she said. And Jesus said, "Neither do I. Go, and sin no more." Jesus showed love and compassion to the woman while at the same time acknowledged her adultery as sin. Whenever people encounter Jesus, His love is evident and He loves us too much to leave us the same way we came to Him. If we are involved in destructive sexual strongholds His Holy Spirit convicts us but never condemns us. Condemnation is from our adversary—satan. Conviction invites us to repent, turn from our sin, receive forgiveness and walk in a new direction. Condemnation is bondage and conviction offers us freedom.

There are some sexual sins that may be perpetrated on us like rape and incest that we never consented to. These situations can leave us with deep wounds in our souls. They can also create negative soul ties. The victims of these cruel acts may erect a fortified wall in their minds as a form of protection. The enemy uses a negative situation such as rape or incest to keep women rehearsing the hurt, nursing the hurt and stuck in a cycle of deep emotional and psychological pain. God can heal the deepest pain as we release it to Him. This is not easy work, but necessary work for us to engage in so we can move past the offenses.

Whether the sexual stronghold was perpetrated on us or something we have chosen the solution can be found in God alone. If we are serious about becoming all God wants us to become we must look the negative strongholds square in the face and be honest with ourselves and with God; we must do the work and move forward. He is willing to heal us and send people to help us heal.

If you are struggling with sexual strongholds and or negative soul ties, please speak with a pastor, a pastoral counselor or a trained therapist, and most of all seek the shelter of our Father God, His Word and His grace, and discover His deep and abiding love for you just as you are. He will free you and heal you.

Strategies We Can Use to Deal With Dream Killers

1. Identify your specific dream killers. Name them one by one. Lay them on the altar once and for all. Jesus already nailed them to the cross over 2,000 years ago.

2. Decide to rid yourself of the dream killers in your life. As you seek God and He shows you what's hindering you, be willing to quickly walk in obedience. God wants to establish

us in truth, and as our hearts become more established in the truth of the Word of God, we will spend less time struggling and battling sin and more time in fellowship with the Father. The Christian life will become "easy and light." For example, as God shows us that sleeping around is hindering us, we must be willing to immediately get out of that bed and leave shame and guilt behind. Jeremiah 33:3, NKJV says, "Call to me, and I will answer you, and show you great and mighty things, which you do not know."

3. Go to God for clarity. Fast and pray until you hear clearly. Stay in a spirit of prayer. Ask yourself: "Have I sought God earnestly about what's hindering me?" The Bible says, "He is a rewarder of those who diligently seek Him." (Hebrews 11:6b, NKJV) Sometimes we must turn over our plates for a while. Sometimes we've got to praise Him and get into His presence. Sometimes we've got to pray until we get an answer. Sometimes we might need to give up something, like TV, social media or complaining, or there may be something specific for you that's separating or preventing you from seeking God.

4. Use the Word of God to defeat the dream killers. Truth always trumps fact. Use specific scriptures. The Bible says in James 4:7, NIV, "Submit yourselves, then, to God. Resist the devil, and he will flee from you." Remember, words have power. Use the Word of God to resist the enemy and also resist Him with the words that you speak every day.

5. Surrender control of your life to the Creator God. Am I entangled? "…let us also lay aside every encumbrance and the sin which so easily entangles us, and let us run with endurance the race that is set before us…." (Hebrews 12:1, NASB) Sometimes we must shed some things in our life in order to

run the race God has before us, accomplish His purpose and fulfill the dreams and visions He has put in us. There are also some pet sins we nurse and continue to pursue that God wants us to stop. There may be relationships we must shed. Ask God what are the weights and sins that entangle us and keep us stuck? What keeps us from walking in total freedom with God?

6. Make a specific plan to be free of the negative or destructive strongholds in your life. Implement your plan with the help of God. Get a journal and deal with every stronghold God reveals.

7. After God has revealed your strongholds and given you a strategy to deal with them, face the dream killers in the power of the Holy Spirit. Don't allow fear to overtake you. "For God hath not given us the spirit of fear; but of power, and of love, and of a sound mind." (2 Timothy 1:7, KJV).

8. Place our faith totally in God, the Dream Giver. In whom/where am I placing my faith? Is my faith in the stock market? Is my faith in my dead loved ones? Is my faith in my job and position? Is my faith in me, and my ability to pull myself up by my bootstraps? The Dream Giver can be trusted, He is a faithful God. We just have to step outside our comfort zone.

9. Find a church home and become part of the body of Christ. "The righteous will flourish like a palm tree, they will grow like a cedar of Lebanon; planted in the house of the Lord, they will flourish in the courts of our God." (Psalms 92:12-13, NIV) When believers are not planted, or rooted and established in a church family, it's an uncomfortable place to be. Being attached to a local church brings blessings. There are no perfect churches. Ask God to plant you where you need to be planted. There is a benefit in being planted. We

believers are the church. It is not a building. Don't get hung up on that. Getting a good word regularly in our local church strengthens us. The Word of God will allow us to face our fears and give us new language to speak over our lives.

10. With the help of a trained Christian counselor or pastor: (a) repent of sin, (b) ask for forgiveness of sins, (3) forgive people who have sinned against you, (4) renounce the enemy and break any yoke of bondage he has on you, (5) take authority over strongholds and all the power of the enemy, (6) receive the release, and (7) confess, "I am totally delivered."

Jesus was very clear on His purpose and the vision He was sent to accomplish while on earth. He came to redeem humankind and reconcile people back to God. When He was getting ready to start His earthly ministry, He began with a forty day fast in the wilderness. While He was there the devil came to tempt Him and distract Him from His purpose. The verses below help us gain a clearer picture of His purpose.

"For I have come down from heaven to do the will of God who sent me, not to do my own will." (John 6:38 NLT) "For God loved the world so much that he gave his one and only Son, so that everyone who believes in him will not perish but have eternal life. God sent his Son into the world not to judge the world, but to save the world through him." (John 3:16-17, NLT). *ĩFor God made Christ, who never sinned, to be the offering for our sin,* so that we could be made right with God through Christ." Cor. 5:21, NLT) "The thief's purpose is to steal and kill and destroy. My purpose is to give them a rich and satisfying life." (John 10:10, NLT)

The purpose of Christ and the schemes of the enemy are diametrically opposed. When we are on the path to do as God has called us to do, the enemy will try to stop the plan. Imagine the King of

Glory being confronted by the devil in the wilderness. He tried to use deception with Jesus but it didn't work.

The Message Bible gives us a good look at the scene in the wilderness:

> *The Devil, playing on his hunger, gave the first test: "Since you're God's Son, command this stone to turn into a loaf of bread." Jesus answered by quoting Deuteronomy: "It takes more than bread to really live."*
>
> *For the second test he led him up and spread out all the kingdoms of the earth on display at once. Then the Devil said, "They're yours in all their splendor to serve your pleasure. I'm in charge of them all and can turn them over to whomever I wish. Worship me and they're yours, the whole works." Jesus refused, again backing his refusal with Deuteronomy: "Worship the Lord your God and only the Lord your God. Serve him with absolute single-heartedness."*
>
> *For the third test the Devil took him to Jerusalem and put him on top of the Temple. He said, "If you are God's Son, jump. It's written, isn't it, that 'he has placed you in the care of angels to protect you; they will catch you; you won't so much as stub your toe on a stone'?"*
>
> *"Yes," said Jesus, "and it's also written, 'Don't you dare tempt the Lord your God.'" That completed the testing. The Devil retreated temporarily, lying in wait for another opportunity. (Luke 4:3-13, MSG)*

Each time satan confronted Jesus, Jesus responded with the Word of God. He was quoting scripture from the book of Deuteronomy in the Old Testament. The Word is a very powerful tool when confronting the enemy. The enemy is the unseen hand behind many of the

Dream Killers in our lives. If the enemy tried to thwart the purposes and plans of God by confronting Jesus, just know the enemy will confront and try to distract us, too. Like Jesus we must be ready to respond with the Word of God.

Since negative strongholds are fortified with lies, we must start with the truth to demolish them. Find as many scriptures as possible to confront the lies.

Questions:

1. What keeps you from pursuing and realizing all your God-given dreams?
2. Who do you need to forgive in order to move forward?
3. Are you willing to confront your Dream Killers?

What Are Your Dream Killers?

In this space, list every Dream Killer you have. By listing them, we are symbolically nailing them to the cross.

He canceled the record of the charges against us and took it away by nailing it to the cross. (Colossians 2:14, NLT).

Therefore we also, since we are surrounded by so great a cloud of witnesses, let us lay aside every weight, and the sin which so easily ensnares us, and let us run with endurance the race that is set before us, looking unto Jesus, the author and finisher of our faith, who for the joy that was set before Him endured the cross, despising the shame, and has sat down at the right hand of the throne of God. . (Hebrews 12:1-2, NKJV)

Things to Remember From Chapter 1

1. Negative words have the power to kill our dreams. We must speak life over every dream no matter what it looks like. (Proverbs 18:21, James 3:6-10)
2. Unbelief kept the Israelites from realizing the promises God had for them. When we don't believe God, it keeps us from all the possibilities God has for us. (Hebrews 4:6)
3. Procrastination keeps us from realizing the dreams within. We must act on what God shows us. (Proverbs 24:30-34, 27:1, 13:4)
4. Victim thinking is a dream killer. It keeps us from taking responsibility and being empowered to move forward. Someone else is always to blame as to why we can't realize the dreams God has given us. This type of thinking keeps us stuck. (John 5:6-8)
5. Unhealthy relationships many times render us unable to move forward. Some of the unhealthy relationship dynamics we may get wrapped up in involve approval addiction, validation issues, control issues and attention-seeking.

6. Busyness and living other people's dreams keep us occupied and focused on the wrong things. In order to move forward with the specific dreams, visions and callings God has given us, we must focus on Him and make Him and His plan for us a priority. (Luke 14:33, 11:41-42, 9:62)

7. Sometimes we fall into illness and addiction because of stress and lack of self-care. Sometimes we suffer an attack by the enemy, and other times there's a life management issue. An unhealthy lifestyle will keep you from your dreams. (I Peter 2:24, Isaiah 53:4, Psalms 103:2-3)

8. Strongholds are what we erect in our minds to fortify or defend a personal belief, ideas and opinions (human reasoning) both good and bad, even if it is a lie. The lie must be demolished with the truth of the Word. The mind is the battleground where the enemy plants ideas and opinions counter to God's truth. (2 Corinthians 10:3-5)

9. The Word of God is one weapon that can be used to demolish negative strongholds. The other weapons are prayer, fasting and praise. (Hebrews 4:12, 2 Chronicles 20, Matthew 6:7-13, 16-18)

10. Some of the destructive strongholds we deal with regularly include unforgiveness, guilt, shame, condemnation, rejection, fear and sexual immorality. (Matthew 6:14, Romans 8:1, Isaiah 53:10, Ephesians 1:6, 1 Peter 2:4-8, 2 Timothy 1:7, 1 Corinthians 6:18-20)

11. We must identify and confront our dream killers, whatever they are. The enemy of our souls will try to keep us from fulfilling the purpose, dreams and visions God has given us. He tried to thwart Jesus's purpose while He was in the wilderness and throw Him off track from the beginning. (John 6:38, 10:10, 4:24)

12. We must have a strategy for prayer to be able to walk in the purpose God has for us. We must be vigilant and intentional and never quit, both praying diligently and working to fulfill our dreams. Many people are attached to our destinies. When we don't walk in our purpose, other people miss out on what God wants to do for them. (Jeremiah 29:11-13)

PRAYER

Dear God,

Thank You for showing me some of the hindrances to the dreams You have placed in me. As I ponder every dream killer in my life, I submit each one to You. I name them one by one [name each dream killer]. I lay them at the foot of the cross. I believe You died for every sin I have and will ever commit. I want to walk unencumbered into the destiny You have for me. Keep me, O God, from operating out of fear and unbelief. I trust You to help me to be free from any bondage that keeps me stuck. When I want to speak negative words and act like a victim, please remind me I can choose differently. When I want to put things off and procrastinate, convict my heart and help me see someone is waiting for me to be faithful and keep moving forward. God, when I want to get involved or continue in an unhealthy relationship, show me a better way and give me the courage to choose differently and wisely. Lord, help me to make the dream You placed inside me a priority and help me to stop being involved in unfruitful activities. Help me to live a healthy lifestyle and recognize stress when it interrupts what You have for me. O God, I can do none of this without Your help. In the midst of so many dream killers, thank You, Lord, for protecting and delivering me from destructive strongholds.

In Jesus's Name,
Amen.

CHAPTER 2

THE DREAM GIRL - OUR IDENTITY IN CHRIST

God made us spirit, soul and body. Many of us spend an inordinate amount of time dealing with what is on the outside of us. How we look is big business. Our hair, our nails, our bodies and our overall image is carefully managed daily, but no matter how much effort we put into maintaining our bodies, they're getting older every day and headed to the grave. Our bodies are our world-consciousness. We put up all kinds of fronts to the world to look good. Our soul gives us our self-consciousness. This part is all about "us," our emotions and what we feel, our mind and what we think, our will and what we want. We spend a lot of time saying to everyone, "it's all about me." But our soul is the part of us that must be renewed daily and restored.

The spiritual part of us, known as our God-consciousness, is where God lives when we allow Him to take control of our lives. Many times being made of three parts causes us to be in conflict within ourselves. At times our world consciousness and our self-consciousness are both in conflict with our God-consciousness, so much so that we don't really know who we are. When we don't know who we are, it is difficult to find our purpose and walk in our purpose. At times we feel like imposters, or hypocrites, at best.

When the world wants to know the identity of a child, it looks to the father of the child to help determine the child's paternity. Ninety-nine point nine percent of the time, a DNA blood sample from the father will determine if the child is his. (FindLaw.com) When we believers want to know who we are, when we want to know our true identity, we must go back to our heavenly Father. God made us. If we had a Mercedes and needed to know something about how it was made and how to maintain it, we would not look in a Lexus manual to see what to do for a Mercedes. If we want to understand our identity, we must go back to the owner's manual, the Bible. The Good Book has so much information about our identity we cannot cover it all in these pages. It's all in the owner's manual. Many of us tend to look at portals like fashion magazines, television, social media, the internet and other sources to determine our identity. But let's glean some insight into what our owner—God—and the owner's manual—the Bible—say about our identity.

We Are Fearfully and Wonderfully Made

We were not a surprise. We were not an accident. There was detail put into how we were made. God had a plan for every day of our life. The Psalmist said in Psalm 139:13-16, NLT, "You made all the delicate, inner parts of my body and knit me together in my mother's womb. Thank you for making me so wonderfully complex! Your workmanship is marvelous—how well I know it. You watched me as I was being formed in utter seclusion, as I was woven together in the dark of the womb. You saw me before I was born. Every day of my life was recorded in your book. Every moment was laid out before a single day had passed." Ephesians 2:10, NLT says, "For we are God's masterpiece. He has created us anew in Christ Jesus, so we can do the good things he planned for us long ago."

When we speak poorly of ourselves, we are speaking poorly about God's creation, which is a masterpiece! We were called to do good works. By His Grace, we can walk in these good works. These good works are the purposes of God. Believe it or not, He already has everything ready to roll. We must ask ourselves, are we walking in what He has already prepared? If not, why not? Not only are we fearfully and wonderfully made, He did not make any mistakes about how we came into the world. If we have dark skin, white skin, yellow skin, big bones or small frames, our outer appearance is not all there is to us. We have inward parts that are so precious to God. He looks at our hearts. He rests in our spirits. He specially made us and threw away each mold. We are truly special to God, and He longs to have a relationship with us.

God Knew Us Before Our Time on Earth Began

When the prophet Jeremiah was being called by God, he gave us insight into his calling. He shared how The Lord gave him this message: "I knew you before I formed you in your mother's womb. Before you were born I set you apart and appointed you as my prophet to the nations." (Jeremiah 1:5, NLT) The prophet Isaiah said, "The LORD called me before my birth: from within the womb he called me by name." (Isaiah 49:1, NLT) This is mind blowing that God knew Jeremiah before he was formed in the womb and called Isaiah by name while he was in the womb. Wow!!

God's plan for people starts long before they are born. He watches over every intricate detail and He even determines our name. When we think we have no purpose, just know God's plan is bigger than we could ever imagine. He crafted us with such care. He made us like Him. He called each of us to a high calling. We can choose to say "yes" to Him or we can say "no." It's our choice. Some of us grasp the Call early in life and some of us do so later in life. The main thing is that at some point in our lives we answer the Call, the purpose for which God made us. When we don't answer the Call, we are most miserable. When we answer, we enter and walk in the spiritual/supernatural realm. We walk in purpose. When we live in the natural realm, we experience measures of temporary peace but nothing lasting.

God Has Intentionally Chosen Us and Called Us His Special People

"Even before he made the world, God loved us and chose us in Christ to be holy and without fault in his eyes." (Ephesians 1:4, NLT)

"...you are a chosen people. You are royal priests, a holy nation, God's very own possession. As a result, you can show others the goodness of God, for he called you out of the darkness into his wonderful light." (1 Peter 2:9, NLT)

"Who dares accuse us whom God has chosen for his own? No one—for God himself has given us right standing with himself." (Romans 8:33, NLT)

"We know, dear brothers and sisters, that God loves you and has chosen you to be his own people." (1 Thessalonians 1:4, NLT).

God did not choose us based on our goodness, or our ability to follow the rules. His choice had nothing to do with how good or how bad we would be. God just decided to choose us, and it feels nice to be chosen especially by God. People didn't always pick us to be in the popular group when we grew up. We may have been excluded from certain cliques. Even now as an adult, we may feel like an outsider because of how people ostracize us—cliques continue even into adulthood. But God and you are a majority. If He chose you before the foundation of the world, who are others to reject you? "What then shall we say to these things? If God *is* for us, who *can* be against us?" (Romans 8:31, NKJV)

God Makes Us Righteous

Righteousness has nothing to do with us, but everything to do with God. "For God made Christ, who never sinned, to be the offering for our sin, so that we could be made right with God through Christ." (2 Corinthians 5:21, NLT) "For you O LORD, will bless the righteous; With favor You will surround him as *with* a shield." (Psalm 5:12, NKJV) "For if by the one man's offense death reigned through one, much more those who receive abundance of grace and of the gift of righteousness will reign in life through the One, Jesus Christ." (Romans 5:17, NKJV)

Righteousness is right standing before God. Holiness is right living. We sometimes get confused about righteousness when we think of ourselves. We know that we don't always do the right things. Another way to spell righteousness is D-O-N-E. Christ took on our unrighteousness and gave us His righteousness. What a deal! We do not have to D-O anything to be righteous except say "Yes" to His free gift. We cannot do anything so terrible that He will not make us righteous if we say "yes" to Him. The cross at Calvary is not about what we DO or DON'T do now, it is about Jesus's work being DONE, finished. On the cross, He said, "It is finished." With His work finished, we must begin to call ourselves what God calls us—righteous. When we are saved, His blood makes us righteous. If we can believe and understand the principle of "imputed righteousness," it can transform our lives. Christ gave us His righteousness and we did nothing to deserve it. He gave us a new identity that is immersed in Christ.

We Are Redeemed by the Precious Blood of Jesus

"…knowing that you were not redeemed with corruptible things, *like* silver or gold, from your aimless conduct *received* by tradition from your fathers, but with the precious blood of Christ, as of a lamb without blemish and without spot." (1 Peter 1:18, NKJV) Redemption is free to whoever accepts Jesus as Lord and Savior. Redemption is free but it wasn't cheap. It cost God everything. In fact in Philippians 2:6-8, NLT, it says, "Though he was God, he did not think of equality with God as something to cling to. Instead, he gave up his divine privileges; he took the humble position of a slave and was born as a human being. When he appeared in human form, he humbled himself in obedience to God and died a criminal's death on a cross." Galatians 3:13, NKJV, says "Christ has redeemed us from the curse of the law, having become a curse for us. (for it is written, Cursed is everyone who hangs on a tree."

Redemption means to be bought back. We were purchased with a price and we no longer have to be slaves to sin. We are free in Jesus.

We Are Sealed by the Holy Spirit

We were sealed with the Holy Spirit of promise. In 2 Corinthians 1:21-22, NKJV, it says, "Now He who establishes us with you in Christ and has anointed us *is* God, who also has sealed us and given us the Spirit in our hearts as a guarantee." Ephesians 1:13, NKJV, says, "In Him you also *trusted*, after you heard the word of truth, the gospel of your salvation; in whom also, having believed, you were sealed with the Holy Spirit of promise, who is the guarantee of our inheritance until the redemption of the purchased possession, to the praise of His glory."

Being sealed by the Holy Spirit is a wonderful thing. The Holy Spirit guides us into all truth, and is our internal GPS (Global Positioning System). He is the voice that says, " Turn here, go this direction, stop here, there's a cliff ahead.".... The Holy Spirit will even say, "Wrong turn," and recalculate the distance and say, "Walk this way."

Once you are sealed with the Holy Spirit of Promise, stay in fellowship with Him. The Bible says in Ephesians 4:30, NKJV, "And do not grieve the Holy Spirit of God, by whom you were sealed for the day of redemption." Let's do a context check about grieving the Holy Spirit. Ephesians 4:29, NKJV, the verse right before, says, "Let no corrupt word proceed out of your mouth, but what is good for necessary edification, that it may impart grace to the hearers." Ephesians 4:31-32, NKJV, then says, "Let all bitterness, wrath, anger, clamor, and evil speaking be put away from you, with all malice. And be kind to one another, tenderhearted, forgiving one another, even as God in Christ forgave you." This delineates the things that grieve the Holy Spirit. Always remember who you are. You are sealed by the Holy Spirit. His Spirit is part of your identity.

God Has Gifted All of Us to Be Significant for the Kingdom

He has deposited much in us. 1 Timothy 4:14, NKJV says, "Do not neglect the gift that is in you, which was given to you by prophecy with the laying on of the hands of the eldership." 2 Timothy 1:6, NKJV, says, "Therefore I remind you to stir up the gift of God which is in you through the laying on of my hands." Not only does God plant dream seeds in us, but He gives us the gifting to accomplish the dreams and purposes for which we were born. When God gives us gifts, He doesn't take them back. Romans 11:29, NKJV, says, "For the gifts and the calling of God *are* irrevocable." Thank God we don't all have the same gift. He has a diversity of gifts to expand and advance His Kingdom. Romans 12:6, NASB, says, "Since we have gifts that differ according to the grace given to us, *each of us is to exercise them accordingly...*"

We Are Adopted Into the Family of God

We all need to feel like we belong, and as believers, God has adopted us as His sons and daughters. Being adopted means we are wanted, we are adored, we are celebrated. The scripture tells us about being adopted. Romans 8:15, NASB says, "For you have not received a spirit of slavery leading to fear again, but you have received a spirit of adoption as sons by which we cry out, 'Abba! Father!'" Abba is like saying "Daddy," a term of endearment. Nothing is as wonderful as being included in God's family, and it starts the moment we say, "Yes God! I receive your invitation to be in the family."

Sometimes in life we feel like we don't belong. We don't even like our family and wish we'd been placed in a different one. But God knows our hearts and He stands ready to receive us with unconditional love no matter how we look, behave or react. He loves us just as we are, but refuses to leave us the way we are. He transforms us into the image of His dear Son Jesus Christ. Not only does He transform us into the image of Christ, He transfers us into His Kingdom. Colossians 1:13-14, NIV says, "For he has rescued us from the dominion of darkness and brought us into the kingdom of the Son he loves, in whom we have redemption, the forgiveness of sins."

We are already born in the image of God. God is perfecting us. God came to earth in human flesh in the form of Jesus. His Son humbled Himself while on earth and died a death we should have died. Jesus left heaven and all its splendor. He lowered Himself to earth and gave up heaven for a season on our behalf. Who would do such a thing other than a loving Father? God desires we express humility as we encounter people every day. Our elder brother Jesus shows us a more excellent way of love and humility. Not only is Jesus our brother, He is our friend. He is a friend that sticks closer than a brother. It's all in the family. Being adopted into God's family is awesome!

A Wonderful Royal Priesthood

The priesthood of all believers came about when Christ became a reality and died for the sins of the world. In the Old Testament, the law required that the priest in the temple would sacrifice the blood of animals to satisfy a Holy God. The priest was the mediator, or the one to stand on behalf of the people. Once Christ came, He was not only the perfect sacrificial Lamb, He was also the High Priest, who made the final sacrifice with His own blood. When Christ died, the veil in the temple was ripped from top to bottom. In the Old Testament, only the rabbinical priest went behind the veil once a year to make atonement for the sins of himself and the people. But Jesus makes us into a kingdom of priests. Revelation 5:10, NASB says, "You have made them *to be* a kingdom and priests to our God: and they will reign upon the earth." When the veil was torn, everything changed. This kingdom of priests no longer needed an intermediary to stand between us and God. Jesus became mediator when He offered Himself up on the cross. Jesus perfected us and sanctified us through His blood and satisfied the requirements God had. As a result, we can go directly into the presence of the Lord, for no earthly priest is needed! From the beginning, God wanted a group of people to serve Him as, "a kingdom of priests and a holy nation." (Exodus 19:6, NASB) A kingdom denotes royalty, thus a royal priesthood.

As we pray, ask God to reveal to us our true identity in Him. He is gracious enough to do it. Once we get a real revelation of who we are in God and what's available in Him, we will be a force to be reckoned with for the kingdom of God. When we don't understand our position, when we don't know who we are in Christ, we live way beneath our privileges. But we must remember that we are an anointed people of God who have been called to do great and mighty exploits. We must stay in a mode of prayer, calling on the name of our God. Jeremiah 33:3, KJV, says, "Call unto me, and

I will answer thee, and show thee great and mighty things, which thou knowest not."

God is an awesome God! Sometimes we must remind ourselves of what God says about us and who we are in Him. We must affirm it and say it out loud every day until we get it. One Dream Girl affirmation looks like this:

Dream Girl Affirmation

Today I remind myself of who God says I am.

*I remind myself that God framed the world
with His words. (Hebrews 11:3)
He spoke, and things came into being.
He spoke light and light appeared. (Genesis 1:3)*

I am made in the image of God. (Genesis 1:26) Today I am reminded that life and death are in the power of my own tongue. (Proverbs 18:21) Today I speak life over myself and everyone attached to me. Today I will speak what God says about me. As a believer in Jesus Christ I am sealed with the promise of the Holy Spirit. (Ephesians 1:13) I have the mind of Christ. (1 Corinthians 2:16) I am redeemed and made righteous by the blood of Jesus. (Ephesians 1:7, 2 Corinthians 5:21) I am a new person created in righteousness and holiness. (2 Corinthians 5:17, Ephesians 4:24) God's favor surrounds me like a shield. (Psalm 5:12) I was chosen by God before the foundation of the world. (Ephesians 1:4) God knew me and called me before I was in my mother's womb. (Jeremiah 1:5) I am beautiful because God made me, and His word says I am fearfully and wonderfully made. (Psalm 139:14)

I am the apple of His eye. (Deuteronomy 32:10) His word says He has a plan for me and He has written it down every day in His book. (Jeremiah 29:11, Psalm 139:16) He directs every step I will take today. (Proverbs 20:24, 16:9) God will cause my enemies to be at peace with me. (Proverbs 16:7) I am blessed with every spiritual blessing, and I have great and precious promises in Christ Jesus. (Ephesians 1:3, 2 Peter 1:4) I have been given authority over all the power of the enemy. (Luke 10:19) Today I will remember I've got the power. I can speak to mountains and they must move. (Matthew 17:20) I speak to mountains of frustration, confusion, stress, discouragement, ineffectiveness and inefficiency, and say, "be moved." Today is a good day because the Lord has made it and I will rejoice and be glad in it. (Psalm 118:24) In Jesus's name.

Developing our own affirmation and saying it each day will boost our confidence in who we are in Christ. Not understanding who we are is the biggest reason we do not go after the dreams and purposes set forth in our lives. When we really understand who we are, and whose we are, it makes all the difference in our lives. We have all we need when we have Christ. Sadly, many believers never tap into the vast resources available to help move their dreams, visions and callings forward because they don't have the revelation that we have everything we need in Him. We cannot just have mental access to these truths. We must believe and walk as if we know them, not just think them. We must walk with a confident hope and go to the throne of grace when we are unsure. God will give us help, grace and mercy when we need it. Press in and go to that deep place with God to get a revelation of who we are! We are significant to God.

As we reflect on our identity in Christ, remember and internalize these concepts. If we are believers and belong to Christ and have made a decision to follow Him and give Him Lordship over our lives, then this will make sense. If not, this may be foreign territory. Our identity may still seem fuzzy. When we accept Jesus as Savior, we immediately have a new identity. He makes us a new creation, but salvation in Jesus is a process. There is a beginning point when we say "yes" to Jesus. At that point He saves us from the penalty of sin, which is death and eternal separation from God. He continues to save us from the power of sin every day. We have power over sin. We no longer have to be slaves to sin. Grace is His ability to help us do what we can't do on our own. We cannot save ourselves. In the future when we go to heaven, He will save us from the very presence of sin. There is no sin in heaven.

For those who don't yet know Jesus and have not experienced a new identity, in order to experience this new identity and to be in good standing with God, we must:

1. Admit we are sinners in need of a Savior.
2. Confess our sins to God.
3. Repent and be willing to turn from sin and embrace our new identity in Christ.

The book of Romans can serve as a roadmap for salvation. Some key scriptures:

"For ever since the world was created, people have seen the earth and sky. Through everything God made, they can clearly see his invisible qualities—his eternal power and divine nature. So they have no excuse for not knowing God. Yes, they knew God, but they wouldn't worship him as God or even give him thanks. And they began to think up foolish ideas of what God

was like. As a result, their minds became dark and confused."
(Romans 1:20-21, NLT)

"For everyone has sinned; we all fall short of God's glorious standard. Yet God, with undeserved kindness, declares that we are righteous. He did this through Christ Jesus when he freed us from the penalty for our sins." (Romans 3:23-24, NLT)

"But God showed his great love for us by sending Christ to die for us while we were still sinners." (Romans 5:8, NLT)

"For the wages of sin is death, but the free gift of God is eternal life through Christ Jesus our Lord." (Romans 6:23, NLT)

"If you confess with your mouth that Jesus is Lord and believe in your heart that God raised him from the dead, you will be saved. For it is by believing in your heart that you are made right with God, and it is by confessing with your mouth that you are saved." (Romans 10:9-10, NLT)
"For, 'Everyone who calls on the name of the LORD will be saved.'" (Romans 10:13, NLT)

"For everything comes from him and exists by his power and is intended for his glory. All glory to him forever! Amen." (Romans 11:36, NLT)

Things to Remember From Chapter 2

1. God knows us. He knew us before we were in our mother's womb. We are not strangers to Him. We are known by God. (Jeremiah 1:5, Isaiah 49:1)
2. God made us. He made us with such intricate detail. We are fearfully and wonderfully made. He knit us together (fashioned us) in our mother's womb. (Psalm 139:13-18)
3. God chose us. He chose us before the foundation of the world. (Ephesians 1:4, 1 Peter 2:9, 1 Thessalonians 1:4)

4. God redeemed us. He redeemed us with His precious blood, so we no longer have to be slaves to sin. We are free! (1 Peter 1:18)

5. God made us righteous. The righteousness is not dependent on anything we've done. He clothes us in righteousness just because. He gives us His righteousness. (2 Corinthians 5:21, Romans 5:17)

6. God sealed us. He sealed us with His Holy Spirit as a guarantee of things to come. The Holy Spirit is our internal GPS. He guides and directs every step. (2 Corinthians 1:21-22, Ephesians 1:13)

7. God adopted us. He adopted us into the family of God. We are heirs and joint heirs with Christ. We have all the rights and privileges of sons and daughters. (Romans 8:15)

8. God gifted us. He gives each of us gifts to be used to advance and expand His kingdom. (Romans 11:29, 1 Timothy 4:14)

9. God made us a royal priesthood. The priesthood of all believers allows us to go directly to God in Jesus's name without an earthly intermediary. We can go into an intimate place of worship and sacrifice to God anytime we like. (Revelation 5:10, Exodus 19:6)

Prayer

O God, I am eternally grateful for Your love and kindness toward me. Thank You for making me the way You made me. When I am tempted to complain about my complexion, my hair, my smile, my body and/or my intellect, help me to remember I am fearfully and wonderfully made by You. I am Your masterpiece. I appreciate You revealing to me my true identity. I am glad to be Your daughter and glad that I am redeemed by Your blood. I declare today I am chosen, gifted, special, righteous and adopted. When I forget who I am in You Lord, remind me. Thank You, God, for Jesus who makes my life possible. Thanks for choosing me and sealing me with Your Holy Spirit. I believe the Holy Spirit leads me, teaches me, comforts me and gives me power to accomplish every dream You have placed in me.

In Jesus's name,
Amen.

In light of who God says we are, spend some time on the identity chart and write down your identity. Use words, drawings or whatever you need to say to affirm who you are.

Who Are You?

Identity Chart

CHAPTER 3

THE DREAM GIVER –
THE CHARACTER OF GOD

Where do dreams come from? Where do they originate? How do they find their way into our minds and ultimately our hearts? How do they become our passion and/or our driving force? When do they become the thing we will die for? The Reverend Dr. Martin Luther King, Jr., back in 1963, on a hot August day, said that he had a dream. His dream was about a society that treated people fairly based on character and not based on skin color. Where did his dream originate? Was it his own dream, or did these ideals originate from a higher place than himself? He did not focus all of his energy on why but found himself asking why not. Why can't this dream be the reality in which I live? By asking why not, Dr. King had tapped into his calling and purpose for being on earth. Although his life was short, it was long enough to fulfill his purpose. His purpose was not for himself alone; his purpose was to have an impact on millions of lives and ultimately change the course of history. His dream came from the Dream Giver, The Creator of Heaven and Earth, the God of the Universe. Dr. King heard the call and answered with an affirmative yes. He took up the mantle and became the drum major for justice for his generation and generations to come.

So why don't we all have lofty ideals and dreams like Dr. King and pursue them? Does God, the Dream Giver, only give dreams and purpose to special people? No. Every person is born with a purpose. God places within every person a gift, dream, vision or calling before they enter earth's atmosphere. Many of us never seek or realize our God-given dreams. Instead of following the dreams and visions God places deep within us, we chase the American Dream. The American Dream is about fame, fortune and the accumulation of wealth. Living large in suburbia, or uptown, appears to be a worthy goal, but many times we find ourselves trapped and overwhelmed with the chase. The American Dream is steeped in entitlement, independence and self-reliance. Our God-given dreams and the American Dream are often miles apart. The latter is driven by our need to get ahead, false security and sometimes greed. The former is driven by a desire to please God, to expand the kingdom of God and to meet the needs of someone other than ourselves. The American Dream has insidiously taken people off the path of their God-given dreams. We pick professions based on making a big salary only to find out money does not satisfy our deep longing to walk in our true purpose. We wonder why the world around us seems like such a hopeless place. When we do not walk in our purpose and fulfill God's dream for us, we find ourselves in a hopeless place. The Bible says, "Hope deferred makes the heart sick, but a dream fulfilled is a tree of life." (Proverbs 13:12, NLT) When we walk in purpose, we feel alive.

When someone is made for a certain purpose and then is used otherwise, it can be labeled as misuse or abuse. For example, children are a blessing from God. They are to be nurtured and brought up to acknowledge their Creator and live a healthy, wholesome childhood. We as parents are to bring them up in the way they should go and when they are old, they will not depart from it. (Proverbs 22:6) If the child is touched or handled in any way differently than what was purposed for them as a child, it is misuse or abuse. When we go down ungodly paths knowingly or even unknowingly, the end result is the same: We feel beaten down, hopeless, misused and abused. We long for so much more. Every person on earth has a purpose and they must not stop until they find it. We were never made for abuse or misuse.

Many people do not even know to pursue their God-given dreams. The American Dream is the only dream they have heard of. But when we discover our God-given dreams, visions and callings, we will move with precision and passion toward our destiny. The good thing about pursuing our God-given dreams is that God gives us free will, and the bad thing about pursuing our God-given dreams is that God gives us free will. We can choose God's path or we can choose our own path. It's up to us. No one makes us move toward the destiny God has for us. Will we do what God desires for our lives or will we make our own way and path? Certainly it is dependent on whether we trust God of not. If we are willing to take a leap of faith and trust God, the reward for that risk will be life changing. If we are willing to abandon our pursuit of the American Dream and follow hard after our God-given dreams, the payoff is rewarding and beyond anything we could imagine.

If we use our free will and choose correctly by following God's plan, we will not only have an impact on history but eternity. The Dream Giver has an amazing plan for our lives. He knows the end from the beginning. The Bible says, "Remember the former things long past, For I am God, and there is no other; *I am God*, and there is no one like Me, Declaring the end from the beginning, And from ancient times things which have not been done, Saying, 'My purpose will be established, And I will accomplish all My good pleasure." (Isaiah 46:9-10, NASB) He made us and He has a plan for us, but he gives us the choice to walk in His plan or not.

God loves us and has incredible thoughts about us. Jeremiah 29:11, NKJV. says, "For I know the thoughts that I think toward you, says the LORD, thoughts of peace and not of evil, to give you a future and a hope." He designed every person so uniquely that we all have our own fingerprints and DNA. God has a purpose for every person born into this world. Many times our purpose is intertwined with a seed He has planted deep within us. The seed may be a dream, a vision or a calling. As we answer the call and move forward with the dreams and visions He gives us, it propels us into our purpose and destiny. Our lives all begin with God and what we decide in this life will determine whether it will end with God.

Everyone created by God started with the very breath of the Creator. Without breath, no one gets to live. God breathed life into us. He is the giver of life. The Bible says, "Then the Lord God formed man from the dust of the ground and breathed into his nostrils the breath *or* spirit of life, and man became a living being" (Genesis 2:7, AMPC). When we took our first breath, God ordained it. His very breath means life to us. Not only did He give us breath but He designed every intricate detail about us. He designed us when we were in our mother's womb. The Psalmist says we are fearfully and wonderfully made. "You made all the delicate inner parts of my body and knit me together in my mother's womb. Thank you for making me so wonderfully complex! Your workmanship is marvelous—how well I know it. You watched me as I was being formed in utter seclusion, as I was woven together in the dark of the womb. You saw me before I was born. Every day of my life was recorded in your book. Every moment was laid out before a single day had passed. How precious are your thoughts about me, O God. They cannot be numbered! I can't even count them; they outnumber the grains of sand! And when I wake up, you are still with me!" (Psalm 139:13-18, NLT)

His workmanship is marvelous! When He made us, He also created good works for us to walk in ahead of time. Ephesians 2:10, NASB, says, "For we are His workmanship, created in Christ Jesus for good works, which God prepared beforehand so that we could walk in them." He has a wonderful plan for our lives. God wrote down the plan for our lives in His book. "…all the days ordained to me were written in your book before one of them came to be." (Psalm 139:16, NIV) We can trust His plan.

God saw us before we were born. Not only did He see us, He also knew us. The prophet Jeremiah gives us insight into this. When Jeremiah first heard God's voice regarding his destiny, this is what he heard the Lord say: "The LORD gave me this message: 'I knew you before I formed you in your mother's womb. Before you were born I set you apart and appointed you as my prophet to the nations.'" (Jeremiah 1:4-5, NLT)

Conception is truly a miracle. Every person on the earth is formed in the womb by God. The womb is holy ground. God Himself came through the womb of a woman in the person of Jesus Christ. The birth of a child is very precious. Not only does God form us, but He knows us. He knows us better than we know ourselves. He had a specific assignment for Jeremiah and He has a specific assignment for us. We are here on earth appointed and assigned to do something special in this generation. When we allow that truth to sink in, then we can begin to understand our purpose and begin to walk in our destiny. Some people come to this realization early in life and others come to that realization much later. Sometimes we spend a lifetime searching for our purpose and some people never find it during their lifetime. When we seek the Dream Giver, we will find our God-given purpose and understand that it is all connected to Him. We have no purpose outside of God.

Not only did God know us before we were in the womb, He

made us in His image and gave us dominion. The Bible says, "And God said, Let us make man in our image, after our likeness: and let them have dominion over the fish of the sea, and over the fowl of the air, and over the cattle, and over all the earth, and over every creeping thing that creepeth upon the earth. So God created man in his own image, in the image of God created he him; male and female created he them." (Genesis 1:26-27, KJV)

We are made in the image of God, which means we are the representation and the manifestation of God in the earthly realm. He made no other creature like mankind. The image of God is multifaceted and not one dimensional. God is sovereign, which means He has supreme authority and rules over everything. One of the root words in sovereign is *reign*. He made us multifaceted, not one dimensional, and He gave us dominion over the earth and everything in it. His initial intent was for us to rule and reign over everything He had made.

Then the fall of man took place in the Garden of Eden, when Adam and Eve ate from the forbidden tree, the tree of the knowledge of good and evil. This one act of disobedience caused mankind to lose that intimate fellowship with God. Satan became known as the god of this world and prince of this world. He has ruled and blinded the minds of people for centuries. When Adam and Eve sinned, it separated them from God. Mankind tried to reconcile with God via religion and good works, but it failed. When Christ died on the cross, He restored the relationship with God and regained everything Satan had stolen. The redemptive blood of Jesus was, and is, the only thing that could make atonement for the sins of mankind.

The gospel of Jesus must be revealed to the lost. The Bible says, "But if our gospel be hid, it is hid to them that are lost: In whom the god of this world hath blinded the minds of them which believe not, lest the light of the glorious gospel of Christ, who is the image of God, should shine unto them." (2 Corinthians 4:3-4, KJV) Being made in the image of God means we have dominion, which is an inheritance of the believer. Every dream God placed in us and the destiny He ascribed to us is possible, but we must stand up and be courageous. We must not be afraid to exercise the power and authority that has been given to us. When God made us, dominion is what He had in mind for us. To be in charge of the whole earth is a big job. He placed lots of us on the planet to accomplish His purpose. He is waiting for us to take dominion over what He specifically invited us to do.

Being made in His image is so complex and means even more than just having dominion. Before Adam and Eve sinned in the garden, the Bible says that man would surely die if he ate from the forbidden tree. God cast them out of the Garden and man continued to live physically, but died a spiritual death. Every person born after Adam and Eve was born physically alive but spiritually dead. What a bummer! We are all born spiritually dead and separated from God until we receive Christ. That is our plight in life.

When we receive Christ by faith, then our spirits are quickened and we become alive again. We are then able to discern spiritual things. If we were just physical and spiritual beings, we would not be so complex, but the fact of the matter is God made us three-part beings: spirit, soul and body. 1 Thessalonians 5:23, NKJV, says; "Now may the God of peace Himself sanctify you completely; and may your whole spirit, soul, and body be preserved blameless at the coming of our Lord Jesus Christ."

The Bible says, "God is a Spirit: and they that worship him must worship him in spirit and in truth." (John 4:24, KJV) We, too, are spirits who live in an earth suit called the body, and we have a soul. We must take care of our spirit, soul and body. We nourish our spirits by praying, fasting, praising, reading God's divine Word and obeying His directions. We strengthen our bodies with proper nutrition, exercise and rest. Our souls must be renewed and restored daily in the Word of God and submitted to the spirit. Renewing our souls is the key to realizing our purpose because the mind is constantly all about, "What I think"; the emotions are all about, "What I feel"; and the will is all about, "What I want." Our soul consists of our intellectual, emotional and decision-making capacity. As we renew our minds to think differently, we eventually behave differently. Rather than submitting to the old nature, we have a choice to submit to the spiritual nature. When we come into a true knowledge of Christ and our spirits are resurrected, we are no longer bound by the things our mind, will and emotions lead us to do. We are no longer slaves to sin. We can choose to submit to the Holy Spirit. We are new creations in Christ. At the time of salvation, our spirits are completely saved, although our bodies continue to move toward the grave and our souls must be continually renewed every day.

The Dream Giver puts dreams and visions deep within us. The old nature says we can't do that, it is too big for us and we don't have time. Every person has the same amount of time—twenty-four hours a day. How we use our allotted time is ours to determine. We can spend time wisely or we can squander it. God sometimes chooses busy people to accomplish His purposes. When Jesus picked His disciples, they were all doing something else. When God puts a vision inside of us, it can become active or lie dormant. We can only know our true purpose and calling by the Spirit of God. To the natural man, things of the Spirit seem foolish to him/her. The Bible says, "But the natural man receiveth not the things of the Spirit of God: for they are foolishness unto him: neither can he know them, because they are spiritually discerned." (1 Corinthians 2:14, KJV)

There are many successful people by the world's standards who have money, position, power and/or fame but have no spiritual direction. In essence, some very connected people are totally lost and have no regard for the things of God. Many feel like they have lived their dreams because of their resources and lavish lifestyle, but at the end of this life every person will stand before God and give an account for his or her life. We came into the world with nothing and will leave with nothing. It is very sad when we climb the career ladder and at the end of the climb we realize the ladder has been leaning against the wrong building. Even when the world labels and affirms us as successful, there are times we have a sense of hopelessness. The overwhelming sense of hopelessness is because there is a God-sized hole in all of us. Only God can fill that void. There are not enough vacations, dinners, movies, shopping sprees, spa treatments, money and/or power to fulfill the longing inside of us for something authentic and purposeful. At some point, we must all go back to the Dream Giver and ask, "What is my purpose?" Our purpose is found in God alone and manifested in so many wonderful ways. God is trustworthy. He has so many wonderful characteristics, too numerous to count. Many of these characteristics are revealed in the Names of God. (See end of chapter.) The Dream Giver is omniscient, omnipotent and omnipresent. What an awesome God we have!

Being omniscient means He is all-knowing, all-seeing and all-wise. It is the state of having all knowledge. The Bible speaks of God knowing everything down to the smallest details. It says He sees the sparrow when it falls and cares for it. Not only that, but He knows the number of hairs on our head, and this is a major detail. It also says He knows our thoughts and words before we think or speak them. Amazing! It even says He knows our very hearts. He saw us in the womb and knit us together. He knows the end of history before it occurs. Since the Dream Giver knows all this, we can trust His plan.

Being omnipotent means the Dream Giver is all powerful. He has power over all things and in all ways and at all times. One of the most powerful things He did was to speak creation into existence. Not only did he speak it into existence, but He has maintained it from the beginning. The earth, moon, sun and stars are still in place, suspended in the universe. He has power over Satan, over kings and kingdoms and governments. His power is not limited to anything. He even has power over death. His Son laid His life down and God raised Him from the dead. What a powerful God! No one can do what he does.

The Dream Giver is omnipresent. He is present everywhere at all times. He is present when we are not aware of Him being present. In every situation we encounter, God is present. He may not intervene and manifest in every situation, but He is present. We cannot hide from God. He is in the darkness and He is in the light. Night and day make no difference to Him, for they are the same. He is even in the tiniest molecule. The Psalmist says, "I can never escape from your Spirit! I can never get away from your presence!" (Psalm 139:7, NLT)

Since the Dream Giver is all-knowing, all-powerful and always present, we can trust Him. When He gives us a dream, He is there to help us carry it out. He wants us to trust Him and surrender to His plan. Dr. King could have said no to God's plan for him because he was a pastor, a husband and a father of four little children and didn't have time. But instead he chose God's plan, which propelled him into the destiny for which he was made. It was a God-sized task. Had Dr. King said no, we may not have ever heard of him, nor celebrate the third Monday of January as a national holiday in his honor. God has so many dreams and visions that have not been activated. He is waiting for us to say "yes." A total yes activated by faith moves the dream forward.

The Dream Giver is loving, kind and giving. The entire Bible is a love story about a God who loves us more than we can understand. He loves us more than we love ourselves. He goes to all lengths to reconcile us back to Himself. He sent Christ to die in our place. That sacrificial death was for all mankind for all times. He gave the most precious gift—His Son. God wants a relationship with us. He loves us, period. The Bible says, "But God showed his great love for us by sending Christ to die for us while we were still sinners." (Romans 5:8, NLT) His love is not dependent on us having it all together or being perfect. He loves us in our mess, our mistakes and our misgivings. All He wants us to do is accept and receive His love. When we receive His love totally, we can't help but to love Him back. He pursues us like the hound of heaven. He pursues us until we draw our last breath on earth. He never gives up on us.

Unconditional love is what God is known for. We can never do anything so terrible that God does not love us. We cannot do things so well to make God love us any more than He already does. He loves us! His love is too deep for us to comprehend. Paul prayed this prayer for the Ephesian Church and I pray this prayer for everyone who needs to experience God's love: "When I think of all this, I fall to my knees and pray to the Father, the Creator of everything in heaven and on earth. I pray that from his glorious, unlimited resources he will empower you with inner strength through his Spirit. Then Christ will make his home in your hearts as you trust in him. Your roots will grow down into God's love and keep you strong. And may you have the power to understand, as all God's people should, how wide, how long, how high, and how deep his love is. May you experience the love of Christ, though it is too great to understand fully. Then you will be made complete with all the fullness of life and power that comes from God." (Ephesians 3:14-19, NLT)

Not only does the Dream Giver love and show kindness, He is merciful, gracious, just and compassionate. Lamentations 3:22-23, NIV, says, "Because of the Lord's great love we are not consumed, for his compassions never fail. They are new every morning: great is your faithfulness." What an amazing God we serve. The Bible also says, "…I will be gracious to whom I will be gracious, and will show compassion on whom I will show compassion." (Exodus 33:19, NASB) God is all seeing and He metes out compassion, and He is also a God of justice. He is a just God. He is not ignorant of what goes on within our world. It may seem some people get away with things, but one day justice will be served. But even in His justice, God still makes room for us to be forgiven. If mankind repents, God will forgive. Forgiveness is one characteristic God values very much. The Bible teaches that God forgives us and He empowers us to forgive others. He adds a condition to this, however: If we don't forgive others, he will not forgive us. We all love to be forgiven when we have found ourselves in the wrong.

The Dream Giver is a forgiver and can be trusted. He is a loving Father who wants an authentic relationship with us. He wants us to work out the awesome plan He has for our lives. The caveat is, we must say yes. Every person who has done anything great for the kingdom of God has had to wrestle with whether they would give God a total "yes." Many of us still struggle. God is not mad at us for struggling, He just knows the sooner we get on with the original plan that more lives will be affected as a result. God-given dreams are not about us, they are about having an impact on a larger world community. When Christ came as an infant into this world, His purpose was to save mankind. He prepared for His assignment for thirty years. Then He came on the scene and spent three years modeling the Way and teaching His disciples. It was a difficult assignment to be crucified on behalf of others, but He stayed focused on the bigger plan. His plan for us is so much bigger than our little plan.

Many years ago I believe God placed a dream in me to have an impact on women in a positive way, and thus God downloaded the idea for a Woman's Empowerment Workshop. It was a wonderful time of learning, inspiration and experiencing the power of God. I put the workshop on the shelf for several years as I worked in the marketplace. My heart and passion for this never went away. I have had a stellar nursing career, and the gifts of healing, nurturing and leadership were just some of the gifts God gave me. He placed a desire within me to minister in a dynamic way, giving people real hope and handles on how to release their God-given dreams/visions and make them realities. I have had to go back to the Dream Giver and ask God to give me insight on how to take the Dream Girl movement to the world..

We must understand that a God-sized dream/vision is the only way to go. If we can do it ourselves, then it is our dream. When it is from God, it is authored by the One who spoke the world into existence, and we need God to accomplish it. He gives us the faith to see dreams and visions through to fruition. Hebrews 12:2, KJV, says, "Looking unto Jesus the author and finisher of our faith; who for the joy that was set before Him endured the cross, despising the shame, and is sat down at the right hand of the throne of God." This reminds us that Jesus is the author and finisher of our faith, but still went by the way of the cross. It was not an easy road to accomplish the purpose of God. The purpose, dreams and visions He has given us may not always appear easy, and in fact they may feel like a cross. But the beauty of our journey is the fact that Jesus has already endured the cross. We don't have to! He has given us grace, which is His ability to be able to do what we cannot do on our own.

When we look at our dreams, visions and purpose, we may have to endure some things before they are realized. We must believe He is a rewarder of those who diligently seek Him. The Father is pleased when we reach out in faith. Each dream and vision must be activated by faith. Hebrews 11:6, NKJV, says "But without faith *it is* impossible to please *Him*, for he who comes to God must believe that He is, and *that* He is a rewarder of those who diligently seek Him."

How is our faith ignited? Romans 10:17, NKJV, says, "So then faith *comes* by hearing, and hearing by the word of God." As we renew our minds daily (hearing the word), and have our souls renewed and restored, it is much easier to submit to the Spirit. Romans 12:1-2, NLT, says, "And so, dear brothers and sisters, I plead with you to give your bodies to God because of all he has done for you. Let them be a living and holy sacrifice—the kind he will find acceptable. This is truly the way to worship him. Don't copy the behavior and customs of this world, but let God transform you into a new person by changing the way you think. Then you will learn to know God's will for you, which is good and pleasing and perfect." The Holy Spirit within us will lead us if we ask Him to.

Our Father has given us dominion and authority from the beginning. Access to His authority allows us to walk out our destiny. If we are born-again believers, we can live out the purpose that God has given us. Faith is the key to activate the purpose in our lives.

He has put His Spirit in us. Being directed by the Spirit and being obedient to His promptings are how we live out the purposes that God has for us. He is a loving God who wants only the best for us. When He plants dream seeds in us, potential and possibilities exist beyond our wildest imagination. That means if He plants it—it is HIS! He can be whatever we need Him to be as we birth His dream seeds. God has many names and we can call on the name of the Lord whenever we want to. We can trust in the name of the Lord. The Bible says, "And they that know thy name will put their trust in thee: for thou, Lord, hast not forsaken them that seek thee." (Psalm 9:10, KJV) And Psalm 20:7, KJV, states, "Some trust in chariots, and some in horses: but we will remember the name of the LORD our God." God has many names and each one represents a different characteristic. Select what name you need God to be for you right now. Call on the name(s) of God as you pray.

The Names of God

El Shaddai	The All-Sufficient One
El Elyon	The God Most High
Adonai	Lord Master
El Olam	The Everlasting God
Jehovah-Nissi	The Lord My Banner
Jehovah-Jireh	The Lord Will Provide
Yahweh	Lord Jehovah
Elohim	The Creator
Jehovah-Raah	The Lord My Shepherd
Jehovah-Shalom	The Lord Is Peace
Qanna	Jealous
Jehovah-Rapha	The Lord Who Heals
Jehovah-Shammah	The Lord Is There
Jehovah-Sabaoth	The Lord of Hosts
El Roi	The God Who Sees
Jehovah-Tsidkenu	The Lord Our Righteousness
Jehovah-Mekoddishkem	The Lord Who Sanctifies You

Things to Remember From Chapter 3

1. Remember God is the ultimate Dream Giver.
2. Our purpose is found in God and God alone. (Isaiah 46:9-10)
3. Go after your God-given dreams; anything else will never satisfy.
4. God designed us in His own image and likeness. We are the express representation and manifestation of God on earth. (Genesis 1:26-27)
5. God created us to have dominion and authority on the earth. (Genesis 1:26)
6. God made us complex and very detailed. He even knit us together in our mother's womb. (Psalm 139:13-18)
7. God knew us and called us by name before we were in our mother's womb. (Jeremiah 1:5, Isaiah 49:1)
8. God is a spirit. We are spiritual beings who live in a body and have a soul. The soul is made up of our mind, will and emotion. (John 4:24)
9. We can only know our true purpose and calling by the Spirit of God. (1 Corinthians 2:14)
10. We lost our fellowship with God when Satan deceived Adam and Eve in the garden. Christ regained our relationship with God when Christ died and was resurrected from the dead. We must step up and walk in the authority and dominion He ordained for us from the beginning. (Genesis 3:6-7, 2 Corinthians 5:18-19, 1 Timothy 2:5, Colossians 1:20, 22, Ephesians 2:16)
11. We can choose to activate the dreams and visions inside of us or not. It's our choice.
12. Success by the world's standard is not God's standard. There

is a void in all of us that can only be filled by God…not the American Dream.

13. We can trust God and we can trust His plan for our lives. (Jeremiah 29:11)

14. God has unconditional love for us and is ready to forgive us of anything no matter how depraved we can be. (Romans 5:8)

15. God wants an authentic relationship with us and is able to help us see the big picture.

16. God is the author and finisher of our faith. Faith is the key to activating the dreams within us. (Hebrews 12:2)

17. God has many names and we can call on Him by name. God can be for us whatever we need Him to be.

PRAYER

Dear Dream Giver,

Thank You for Your great love. You have loved me with an everlasting love. You created me with such tender care and intricate detail. Thank You for making me so wonderfully complex. You knew me before time began. You appointed me to do great things in the earth, You even called me by name. I am so grateful that You, O Lord, designed me to walk in purpose and to make a difference for eternity. Help me to not be fearful and allow me to walk with boldness as I am obedient to Your Word. You know the end from the beginning. I expect great things to manifest in my life as I seek to advance the kingdom of God. I ask You to be Jehovah-Nissi, my Victory Banner, as I say yes to the dreams, visions and calling You placed within me. I am excited about walking in dominion, power and purpose. Help me to remember I am made in Your image and I have the ability to be loving, kind, compassionate, gracious, merciful, forgiving and so much more. Thank You for the wisdom of Your word.

In Jesus's name,
Amen.

CHAPTER 4

THE DREAM - PREGNANT WITH POSSIBILITY

There are age old questions that men and women, boys and girls seem to always get around to asking. I call them the destiny questions like: "Why I am here?" Or some ask, "What is my purpose on earth?" "How am I to do what I am called to do?" "Where in the world am I supposed to be right now in my life?" Some ask why, some ask what, others ask how and others ask where. And there is always the timing question, when.

Believers often ask God, "What is Your plan for my life?" I want to pose a better question for those of us who are believers. Instead of asking, "What is Your plan for my life?" the question should be, "God, what is Your plan?" God always has a plan and He is working His plan. He has a plan for each and every one of us, so why don't we find out His plan and connect with Him. God knows the end from the beginning! I want to challenge us to ask God what His plan for us is, but be ready for Him to answer. And when he answers, He's going to rock your world! When we focus our plans on our lives it pales in comparison to God's plan. He wants us to be part of something that will make a difference for the Kingdom of God for this generation and generations to come. In our plan, our hands are cupped. In His plan, his arms are wide open. We focus on our plan, He wants us to focus on His plan.

Many of us are at "half-time" in our lives. If we are thirty-five to forty years old, we most likely have lived the first half of our lives. Many of us have been successful. Success may be that we finished college, own our own home or car, have some money in the bank, started a business, started a ministry and/or had beautiful children. According to author Bob Buford in the book *Halftime,* we need to move from success to significance. My prayer is that we would transform our existence on planet earth by being in the very center of God's will. To create significant transformation in our lives, we must make the best of every day. God used twelve disciples to change the course of history and turn the world upside down. God is looking for someone whose heart is diligent toward Him so He can show Himself to be mighty. God can use one person to change the course of history and do great exploits. Maybe that person is you.

In Jeremiah 29:11, NIV, the Bible says, "'For I know the plans I have for you,' declares the LORD, 'plans to prosper you and not to harm you, plans to give you hope and a future.'" We hear this verse quoted often, but what we don't know is that during this season the Israelites were in Babylonian captivity. Read one verse up and you will discover that it was prophesied that the Israelites would spend seventy years in captivity before God would come and get them. In the meantime, Israel was to relax, build houses, marry and have kids. But God said He had a plan. As I have mentioned earlier, the plan for our lives started before we were born. God has a plan and He has perfect timing. Like the Israelites, many of us are in bondage to something, but God has a hope and a future for us. We are very precious to God!

There are people walking to and fro throughout the earth trying to figure out what their destiny is and what they should do with their lives. They go to fortune tellers, soothsayers and witch doctors. They go to palm readers. They believe in crystals and tarot cards, Ouija boards, psychics, séances and other occult practices. They wander around aimlessly. When people have no purpose, they end up making up things to do as their purpose and they spend time on worthless idols like television, movies, money, power, fame, violence, intellect, traditions, recreation, sex, people and addictions.

When we are void of purpose, getting our nails done is more important than hearing from God. If we the church, His believers, were being what God wanted us to be, which is God's prophetic voice, people would run to the prophet rather than the palm reader. They would go to the teacher rather than to tarot cards. They would go the faithful evangelist rather than the fortune teller. They would go to the pastor rather than the prostitute. They would go to the apostle rather than astrology. People are hungry for a supernatural sign and move of God. The church, God's prophetic voice in this hour, is much like the prophet Jonah. He was to go and preach and prophesy to the city of Nineveh, but he was asleep on a boat going in the opposite direction from where God said to go.

Many churches are asleep and headed in the wrong direction. People need to hear that God has a wonderful plan for their lives found in Jesus Christ. Nothing will ever satisfy the void in us but Jesus. People need to hear that they are not an accident, or a mistake, or illegitimate, that their lives matter and have purpose and there is something greater than themselves. God planned us from the beginning of time. God is never without a plan, for His timing and our timing are different. We think we get ordained for this or that in our timeframe, but God's in charge. God already decided we would be an apostle, evangelist, teacher, pastor, prophet and much more before we were born. God knew Jesus would be the Savior of the world before the world began. John 1:1, NLT, says, "In the beginning the Word already existed. The Word was with God, and the Word was God." Verse 14 says, "So the Word became human and made his home among us. He was full of unfailing love and faithfulness. And we have seen his glory, the glory of the Father's one and only Son."

So if God foreknew what would happen with the Psalmist, every day of his life having been written in His book; and with the Prophet Jeremiah, who was appointed a Prophet before he was born; and with Jesus Christ the Savior of the world, full of grace and truth, why wouldn't He have an awesome plan awaiting our lives too?

Let's look closer at the birth announcement of Christ to glean some insight on conceiving something great and being pregnant with possibility. As we read this birth announcement, think about the dreams, visions, purpose and destiny God has put in your belly. Think of them as dream seeds. Read carefully through the passage in Luke 1:26-45, NKJV:

Christ's Birth Announced to Mary

> Now in the sixth month the angel Gabriel was sent by God to a city of Galilee named Nazareth, to a virgin betrothed to a man whose name was Joseph, of the house of David. The virgin's name was Mary. And having come in, the angel said to her, "Rejoice, highly favored one, the Lord is with you; blessed are you among women!"
>
> But when she saw him, she was troubled at his saying, and considered what manner of greeting this was. Then the angel said to her, "Do not be afraid, Mary, for you have found favor with God. And behold, you will conceive in your womb and bring forth a Son, and shall call His name JESUS. He will be great, and

will be called the Son of the Highest; and the Lord God will give Him the throne of His father David. And He will reign over the house of Jacob forever, and of His kingdom there will be no end." Then Mary said to the angel, "How can this be, since I do not know a man?"

And the angel answered and said to her, "The Holy Spirit will come upon you, and the power of the Highest will over-shadow you; therefore, also, that Holy One who is to be born will be called the Son of God. Now indeed, Elizabeth your relative has also conceived a son in her old age; and this is now the sixth month for her who was called barren. For with God nothing will be impossible."

Then Mary said, "Behold the maidservant of the Lord! Let it be to me according to your word." And the angel departed from her.

Mary Visits Elizabeth

Now Mary arose in those days and went into the hill country with haste, to a city of Judah, and entered the house of Zacharias and greeted Elizabeth. And it happened, when Elizabeth heard the greeting of Mary, that the babe leaped in her womb; and Elizabeth was filled with the Holy Spirit. Then she spoke out with a loud voice and said, "Blessed are you among women, and blessed is the fruit of your womb! But why is this granted to me, that the mother of my Lord should come to me? For indeed, as soon as the voice of your greeting sounded in my ears, the babe leaped in my womb for joy. Blessed is she who believed, for there will be a fulfillment of those things which were told her from the Lord."

Now imagine God asking you to do something great that would have a powerful impact on your generation for all of eternity, and that He sent an angel to say you were chosen for this assignment. Look closely at all the things the angel told Mary. Re-read and underline everything the angel said. In Luke 1:37, NKJV, it says, "For with God nothing will be impossible." That means anything is possible and there are possibilities. We are all pregnant with possibility.

The Angel's Message

"And having come in, the angel said to her, 'Rejoice, highly favored one, the Lord is with you; blessed are you among women!'" Luke 1:28, NKJV

When we are chosen by God to bring forth something great in the world, we must understand where we stand with Him and what our identity in God is. He knew Mary would not feel worthy of this great honor, so He had the angel affirm that she was "highly favored." Not just favored, but highly favored. How many of us believe we are highly favored and blessed? If we belong to God, we are blessed and highly favored. The angel also had to reassure Mary that the Lord was with her. Mary did not alter her looks to stand out from other women, but she was God's choice. When God chooses us, we are special. Like Mary, we are God's chosen woman, man, girl or boy. Unless we understand how favored we are and how blessed we are by God, then we will continue to compare ourselves to other people and also try to get approval from people.

Unfortunately, some people in our lives will always want to see us through their eyes, and only see what we are in the natural; a poor girl from the ghetto is all they allow themselves to see without seeing our true worth or value. Worth and value have nothing to do with where we grew up or where we came from or how much money or education we have. If I crumple up a dollar bill and then throw it on the floor and step on it, does the bill lose its value just because it was balled up and thrown on the floor? No. When our lives take twists and turns, and we feel like a piece of gum on the bottom of someone's shoe, remember worth and value come from God. Our intrinsic value has nothing to do with the difficulties and hard times we have been through. We are valuable because God says we are valuable. Our potential may have gone unnoticed and or untapped. Our dreams and visions may not be embraced by everyone. In fact, people may be negative and skeptical about us, but that does not matter. Only what God believes about us really matters. We must listen to the angels in our lives who affirm us. Mary might have been a poor young girl, but God declared her blessed and highly favored. If God's declares that about us, we should say that about ourselves. We should all say out loud, "I am blessed and highly favored!"

"Do not be afraid Mary for you have found favor with God." (Luke 1:30, NKJV) God knew this would scare the daylights out of Mary, so right off the bat He said do not be afraid. The scripture in the NLT says Mary was "confused and disturbed." The NIV says she was greatly troubled. The Amplified say she was all three: confused, disturbed and "greatly troubled." When God first calls us to something great, we may be disturbed and confused. We say, "I can't believe this is happening to me!" Fear is one of our biggest hindrances to doing kingdom work. Fear is the opposite of faith. When we allow fear to overtake us, we do irrational things. But God said do not be afraid. He said that because He knew the human response to angelic messages would be fear. When we fear, we often talk to ourselves. We say things like: "I don't know if I can pull this off." "What will my family think?" "What will the neighborhood people say?" Or we think, "Will the people on my job respect me and validate my ideas?" We ask ourselves, "Will this work?"

In Linda Willis's book *Pregnant With Potential*, she asks the questions we grapple with when we conceive something great and fear stares us in the face. Sometimes we fear success and sometimes we fear failure. What if [fill in the blank] doesn't work out? What if [fill in the blank] is successful and I can't maintain it? What is God doing in my life? These are some of the things we struggle with when we hear God speaking to us. All these fears are founded upon our own natural ability. But potential born of God goes beyond what we can do on our own because it is conceived by the Holy Spirit. Mary did not need to fear because she had found favor with God. He would be responsible for fulfilling His purpose in her life. We never have to be afraid of the possibility that God will disregard His responsibility. God is not in the business of starting something He can't finish. He does not involve us in something and then disappear, leaving us holding the bag.

Mary probably was thinking about the naysayers of Nazareth. Can you imagine the gossip that spread in the neighborhood about Mary's pregnancy? Remember, everybody is not going to understand or accept what God is doing in our lives. Mary was engaged to be married and then showed up pregnant and said God did it. Not only was she eligible to be stoned for that, but people probably thought she was crazy and blasphemous. But there is nothing to fear when we have the favor of God. Favor protects us from failure. Favor allows us to overcome rejection. Favor assures success.

In Psalm 5:12, NLT, the Psalmist says "For you bless the godly, O LORD; you surround them with your shield of love." God will protect us. "'No weapon formed against you will prosper, And every tongue which rises against you in judgment You shall condemn. This *is* the heritage of the servants of the LORD. And their righteousness *is* from Me,' says the Lord." (Isaiah 54:17, NKJV) Fear is not from God. If we are feeling fearful, just know that according to

2 Timothy 1:7, NKJV, "For God has not given us a spirit of fear, but of power and of love and of a sound mind." When God chooses us for something great, don't be scared! And above all, don't allow fear to turn into disobedience. We should go ahead and put our name in the pot for that promotion; go ahead and write that book; go back to school; move to a new city; stay home with your children; start that Bible study and prayer group; go ahead and start that business. If God calls us to something, stop giving excuses because we are fearful. Step out and just do it.

"And behold, you will conceive in your womb and bring forth a Son, and shall call His name Jesus. He will be great, and will be called the Son of the Highest; and the Lord God will give Him the throne of His father David. And He will reign over the house of Jacob forever, and of His kingdom there will be no end." (Luke 1:31-33, NKJV) "Conceive" is a powerful word. One of the meanings is to "take or receive"; "to take together." Mary would receive the most Holy seed to bear of all humankind. There is only one Savior of the world, but Mary is symbolic of all of us. Every person God calls is pregnant with possibilities and potential. God plants dream seeds. Mary was an ordinary woman from the ghetto of Galilee. She was young. She was unmarried. She was poor. Nothing too special seemingly. Some of us are just like Mary: young; ordinary; poor; unmarried; or some are married, but God has placed something deep within us that must be birthed into the earth. But the story of our Savior is not just about a young woman. It is an old woman, Elizabeth, who conceives too. For those of us who are young at heart but wise in years, God still plants seeds in older women and men too. We may be seasoned, mature, married or unmarried, but God still uses older people. We're never too old to do kingdom business. Like Mary, Elizabeth was to give birth to John the Baptist, who was the forerunner to Jesus. Elizabeth represents all of us who may think we're too old to do anything significant for God. But not so, for we are pregnant with possibility. God can use any earthen vessel to accomplish His purpose. He put His light and Spirit within us. When we have Jesus in us, the possibilities are endless. 2 Corinthians 4:7, NKJV, says, "But we have this treasure in earthen vessels, that the excellence of the power may be of God and not of us." Once we conceive something, growth and maturity of that "baby" starts to happen. Don't abort what God has placed in us. He did not make any mistakes. Go ahead and enjoy the journey; some pregnancies are difficult, but hang in there. God will deliver what you are pregnant with.

Some of us have been pregnant with possibility for years, months and days. We heard clearly what God wants to birth in us, and for some of us it's past time for the delivery to have occurred. Some us are in the labor room right now. Some of us just found out we are pregnant with something. No matter where we are in the gestation process, at some point we must deliver. Our delivery may be like Mary's. We may not have a lot of money, we may have to deliver the baby in modest circumstances and wrap it in swaddling clothes and place it in a manger. The Bible says do not despise small beginnings. Small things with the power of the Holy Spirit can have an impact on the world for eternity. When God ordains something, it will come to pass, and all we have to do is cooperate with His timing and His way of doing things. His ways are not our ways. He will accomplish His purpose even if He has to find another person who is willing to do what He says do.

What's has God placed in your belly? What has He made your passion? What dream is burning inside of you? I believe every person has a dream, every person has a purpose for why God put us here at this time in history. Has God placed in us a sermon, a ministry, a book, a song, a business, a career, a relationship to be cultivated?

God may have gotten you through a failed marriage, and now He wants you to start a divorce recovery ministry. I don't know, but God knows. What I do know is that there is greatness in all of us, and it has to come out. Remember God had one Christ Child, but He may have multiple things He wants to birth in us. If I had stopped dreaming when God accomplished my first dream, I would have stopped dreaming at age twenty-two. Since then He has given me songs, ideas for books, teaching series and so much more. Never stop being available to God because He wants to plant many seeds in us. He is an awesome God!

Luke 1:34-35, NKJV, says, "Then Mary said to the angel, 'How can this be, since I do not know a man?' And the angel answered and said to her, '*The* Holy Spirit will come upon you, and the power of the Highest will overshadow you; therefore, also, that Holy One who is to be born will be called the Son of God.'" Mary asked a good question, a destiny question: How will this be possible since I am a virgin?

But I caution us to not get stuck on how! When God speaks to us and says thus and so, sometimes it is so big it scares us and we get stuck on how. How will we do it? How will God's vision come to pass? So we fail to move forward, and get stuck. Then we say things like, "I don't see how that could happen given what I am seeing now." God doesn't mind if we ask "How?" He just doesn't want us to dwell there too long. Sometimes we get stuck on the small stuff and need to know every turn of every detail. Sometimes this "need to know" keeps us from delivering the greatness, the dreams and the potential that is in us.

I am reminded of another woman who was told she would get pregnant—Sarah. Sarah was in doubt and unbelief, so she decided to "help" God by giving her maidservant Hagar to Abraham to produce a child. The Hagars in our lives are the things we make happen by our force of wills. We may not see how God is going to make things come to pass in our lives since we can't see the end from the beginning as God can. Instead we should decide to be like Mary and trust God with the "how." She came to that point, and said "Behold the handmaid of the Lord; be it unto me according to thy word". (Luke 1:38, KJV)

When God allows us to conceive His plan and purpose, the only way it can come to pass is by the power of the Holy Spirit, who empowers us to do miracles. Things we cannot accomplish in our own strength can be accomplished with the power of the Holy Spirit and with God's grace, which He gives to us. A good definition of grace is this: Grace is God's ability working in man, making him able to do what man cannot do in his own ability. John 1:17 NKJV says, "For the law was given through Moses, but grace and truth came through Jesus Christ." The Old Testament law was truth. Men had tried to keep the law through their own natural ability but couldn't, so when Jesus came, He not only brought truth but gave us a way to live that truth. Grace which is God's ability working in man is the only way to live that truth. When God gives us something big to do, rely on His grace to get it done. His grace truly is amazing.

The power that raised Jesus from the dead is the same power that lives in believers. Romans 8:11, NLT, says, "The Spirit of God, who raised Jesus from the dead, lives in you. And just as God raised Christ Jesus from the dead, he will give life to your mortal bodies by this same Spirit living within you." Who would have thought that nonviolent protesting could change the face of a country? Yet Dr. King proved that in the power of the Holy Spirit, great things could be accomplished. It was not him but it was God. It is not the earthen vessel, but the power of God on the inside. The person that stops the Holy Spirit from working the most is us. 1 Thessalonians 5:19, NIV, says, "Do not quench the Spirit."

Mary was told by the angel that the power of the Highest will overshadow you. Many of us think we have the answer and we try to overshadow the Holy Spirit and take over. Guess what? God allows us free will and room to take over, but if we allow Him to lead, His GPS works much better than our trying to use our map *and* trying to use the Holy Spirit, too.

AFFIRMATION:

I've got the "Power of the Holy Spirit" living inside me.

AFFIRMATION:

God gives me grace to work it out, and to walk it out. "The grace of the LORD Jesus Christ, and the love of God, and the communion of the Holy Ghost be with you all. Amen" (2 Corinthians 13:14, NKJV)

"What's more, your relative Elizabeth has become pregnant in her old age! People used to say she was barren, but she has conceived a son and is now in her sixth month. For nothing is impossible with God. (Luke 1:36-37, NLT)

When people say to us that we are barren, that basically we have not brought forth any fruit, then we say to them, "Nothing is impossible with God." When people pick out certain people and say we are the beautiful ones and you are not the beautiful ones, then we should say, "Nothing is impossible with God." When people say we were born on the wrong side of the tracks and will never amount to anything, we must talk to ourselves and say, "Nothing is impossible with God." Farrah Gray, who wrote the book *Reallionaire,* was a young man born in the impoverished Southside of Chicago who became a millionaire at 14 years old. "Nothing is impossible with God."

The word impossible is found in Luke 1:37 and other places in the Bible. Matthew 17:20, NKJV, says, "So Jesus said to them, 'Because of your unbelief; for assuredly, I say to you, if you have faith as a mustard seed, you will say to this mountain, 'Move from here to there,' and it will move; and nothing will be impossible for you." Matthew 19:26, NKJV, says "But Jesus looked at *them* and said, 'With men this is impossible, but with God all things are possible.'" (Jesus was speaking of a rich man being saved, and the disciples asked who can be saved then?) And Hebrews 11:6, NKJV, states, "But without faith *it is* impossible to please *Him,* for he who comes to God must believe that He is, and *that* He is a rewarder of those who diligently seek Him."

Each one of these verses about impossibilities has to do with faith or lack of faith. Faith is what makes things possible. Jesus said if you have faith, you can speak to mountains in your life and they would move. Jesus said nothing will be impossible. Some of us have impossible, immovable situations in our lives. Begin to say what Jesus said. Agree with His words. Tell the mountain to move and "nothing is impossible." Don't tell God how big our problems/mountains are; instead tell our problems/mountains how big our God is. Jesus again affirmed that, "With men this is impossible, but with God all things are possible."

AFFIRMATION:
With God all things are possible.

In Hebrews it says it is impossible to please God without faith. Our faith is the limiting factor over impossibilities. Our faith must be activated to pull the impossible into the possible. Our faith must be activated to make the invisible visible, to make the intangible tangible. If we are unwilling to move from faith-less to faith-filled, then impossible things will not happen. When God tells us to do something big, too big, it seems, for us to accomplish, step out in faith and He will provide everything we need.

Many people quote Luke 1:37, NLT: "For nothing is impossible with God." In context, this was speaking of an old barren woman who was now six months pregnant. She no doubt had dreamed in her young years to be pregnant and God was faithful to bring this to pass. Her shame would finally be removed. I believe the angel was saying to Mary, "Look! A miracle was already performed six months ago with Elizabeth. We can do anything ordained by God and possibilities are endless. Not only can God use an old woman to show forth His glory, He can use a young woman to bring the most precious gift the world has ever known."

He used a woman to bring Jesus into the world. This is significant. He could have just dropped Jesus from heaven but God used a woman. Women in that culture were not thought of as special and were considered property of men. Jewish men use to pray, thanking God that He didn't make them a woman but a man. But God uses men and women for His glory. Let's thank God He made us a woman, an anointed woman of God who is able to birth things into the earth. Don't underestimate God's ability to get glory from a young woman, a teenager, an old woman, a homeless person, an executive or a man who stays before God in prayer. If God can use a donkey to speak, or an adulterer like David, or a murderer like Moses, or a traitor like Peter, He can use us. Don't let your past keep you from fulfilling the dream God has placed in you from the beginning of time.

Some of you may be thinking, "My life is so jacked up and I have created a lot of it myself." Don't worry. God can handle everything we have messed up. He specialized in putting broken things back together and making them brand new. We must find a way to forgive ourselves and say nothing is impossible with God. Let's not let lack of money or know-how keep us from moving forward. God will send us everything we need. All He asks us to do is say, "Yes."

Mary's response in Luke 1:38, NLT, was, "I am the Lord's servant. May everything you have said about me come true." Even though the angel gave Mary this grand message from God himself, she still had to say yes. In the KJV translation, she said, "...be it unto me according to thy word." This was Mary's way of waving her faith flag. She basically said I have faith that this will come to pass. It will happen. How many of us would have been willing to say yes like Mary? How many will say at your word Lord I am willing. How many of us are willing to launch out into the deep by faith expecting the Holy Spirit to give us direction? I dare us to say, "Yes, I'm willing to do whatever God is birthing in the earth for the kingdom of God through me." God will never force us to receive what He has for us. He gives us all free will. It is our decision to say yes. If our lives are plagued with uneasiness, fear, confusion and/or depression, chances are we are not living within the boundaries of God's best for us. Do like the old people said...have a little talk with Jesus. It will make it right!

In Luke 2:6-7, Jesus was born. "...the days were completed for her to be delivered. And she brought forth her firstborn Son, and wrapped Him in swaddling cloths, and laid Him in a manger, because there was no room for them in the inn." (Luke 2:6-7, NKJV) At some point, the baby must be delivered. Some of us have been pregnant with possibility for ten, twenty and even thirty years.

It is time to give birth! God will send the mid-wives to help us push. Let someone know you are pregnant with possibility and that greatness is about to be born and say "yes" to God today. We may find ourselves asking: "Why am I here?" "What's my purpose?" "How am I supposed to do this?" "Where in the world am I supposed to be?" Go back to the Dream Giver, for He has the answers. Seek Him above everything.

Things to Remember From Chapter 4

1. Remember that God knew you and saw you before you were born and He thinks good things about you and has a wonderful plan for your life. He has already appointed you and anointed you. Remind yourself of this often. (Psalm 139:16)

2. Go to the Father in earnest prayer. Seek Him and *His* plan, not *your* plan for your life. HIS PLAN! (Jeremiah 29:11-13)

3. Affirm every day that you are blessed and highly favored by God. (Luke 1:28)

4. Don't be scared, fear is not of God. He has not given us a spirit of fear but of power, love and a sound mind. (2 Timothy 1:7)

5. Know with assurance that what is conceived in you must come to pass for the Kingdom. Other people's destiny is attached to you.

6. Don't get stuck on how; move when God says move. The Holy Spirit will overshadow you and accomplish the assignment. (Luke 1:35)

7. Nothing is impossible for God, for the word of God will never fail. Trust God for the impossible. (Luke 1:37)

8. Give birth to the dreams God has given so that you fulfill the purposes God has for your life.

9. Be the church. Stop hanging out in our Holy Huddles as others wrestle with the destiny questions and be ready to answer them: JESUS is the answer and the HOLY SPIRIT will give you direction and GOD the FATHER has a wonderful plan for everyone's life. You don't have to turn to counterfeits. God is the real Giver of Dreams.

10. We are never too old or too young to be pregnant with possibility. God can use anyone yielded to Him.

PRAYER

Dear God,

The Giver of worthy dreams, I am so grateful for what You have placed inside me. I am saying yes to You God today. I want to make a difference for the kingdom of God. Allow me to do all You have called me to do and to impact everyone attached to my destiny. Help me to always remember the plan You have for me is Your plan, God, not mine. Help me to give birth to everything You have put in me. I will not be fearful with the guidance of the Holy Spirit. When the dreams and visions are born, remind me to give You all the glory for the great things You have done.

In Jesus's Name,
Amen.

Create some alone time and seek God about the dream/vision/ calling He has for you. Here is a blank sheet for you to answer these questions. Take as much time as you need to write down the dream God has place within you. Later you will have time to rewrite it with specific goals.

What has God placed in your belly?
What has He made your passion?
What dream is burning inside you?

NEVER EVER GIVE UP ON WHAT GOD IS DOING WITHIN YOU!

CHAPTER 5
WRITE THE VISION/DREAM

"Write the vision and make it plain on tablets, that he may run who reads it. For the vision is yet for an appointed time; but at the end it will speak, and it will not lie. Though it tarries, wait for it; because it will surely come, it will not tarry." (Habakkuk 2:2-3, NKJV)

God has a purpose and vision for every life He made. He has a dream for each and every one of us, and He wants us to write down our dreams and visions. In the bible, God told Habakkuk to write down the vision, and write it down large enough so that someone running by would be able to read it! God wants us to keep our dreams visible in front of us so that we don't lose sight of the dream and lose faith. And He also wants others to be able to see and take part in our dreams as well.

Many times we have magnificent dreams, yet no one knows about those dreams but us. Sometimes we even keep our dreams hidden in the recesses of our hearts and minds. But as God speaks His dreams to us, we must write them down; He wants us to document His dreams for us so we can more easily follow and execute them and bring them to pass. Thus we must train ourselves to discern His voice so that we may hear from Him clearly. God writes His plans down for us in His book before we are born. When we hear from God, we should write down what He tells us, because when we write down what He tells us it serves several purposes. First, it reminds us of what God said, and it also it allows us to share His vision with others in our circle to see if said dream resonates with them, so that they too can run with the vision. It also allows future generations to see the goodness of the Lord so that they too can praise Him.

When we read the Word of God as presented at the beginning of this chapter and hear Him speak something significant, we should write it down. Not having a vision for what God says about our life is a problem. Helen Keller once said, "The only thing *worse than being blind* is having sight *but no vision.*"

God has a purpose and vision for every life He made. The Bible says, "Where there is no vision, the people perish…" (Proverbs 29:18, KJV) We don't want people to perish in our generation; we want there to be a fresh vision so that we can all pursue what God says. Psalm 102:18, NASB, says, "This will be written for the generations to come, That a people yet to be created may praise the LORD." The Hebrew word for vision is *chazown*, which means dream, revelation or vision. In the book *Chazown*, by Craig Groeschel, he says, "Where there is no chazown—no dream, no revelation, no vision, no sense of created purpose—we perish."

In order to find our chazown, we must earnestly seek God about where we must go and what we are to do. God already has the plan laid out; all we need to do is tap into Him. When we hear from Him, then we must write down what He says so we can turn His plan into a reality. It does not need to be complicated. Just start with answering the questions that follow. You may use the vision sheet at the end of this chapter to record your answers.

1. What do you believe one of your big God-given dreams is? Be very specific as you write down what you believe God is calling you to do. (Remember: If it's something you can accomplish on your own, then it's probably not your God-given dream.) God may be calling you to start a business or ministry. He may be prompting you to write a book, a play or music. Perhaps you're supposed to help young people get into college, or He wants you to invent something or find a cure for something. Your dream may be to open a home for children or the elderly, or a bed and breakfast for clergy people. The possibilities are endless! Remember nothing is too hard for God.

2. Who do you believe God is calling to help you accomplish your dream/vision? Is it close friends, family or people you've yet to meet? The reality is that when God gives us a big vision/dream, most likely we cannot accomplish it alone. Even when Jesus came to earth to redeem the world, He did not do ministry alone. He chose twelve people, twelve disciples to be apprentices and help Him as He went about preaching, teaching, healing and delivering many. The disciples followed Jesus everywhere and were open to learning. They were not afraid to get involved. He called each one individually and they all had the opportunity to say "yes" or "no." He even chose one who would betray Him! Jesus had lots of different personalities to help Him get the ministry accomplished before He headed to do His ultimate task of being crucified. Some things only Jesus could do, and that was one of them, but there were so many things others did to carry out the will of God. Pray and ask God who He wants to help you get the task accomplished. Once God

reveals to us who the people are, then ask them for help. Be very specific about what you need. Don't be afraid to ask questions and be open to feedback. Sometimes we don't know what we don't know. Pray that God will send folks who will illuminate our blind spots.

3. Where will you give birth to your dream/vision? At home? At work? At your church? At a building you secure? Is your dream to manifest in the city where you are or somewhere else? Will it be fostered in a virtual community online? Is it a global vision? Your dream may start small then expand, or it may start globally—it just depends on what it is.

4. Why is your dream/vision important to the kingdom of God? Ponder this question and seek God for a good answer. If your dream/vision won't make an impact on the Kingdom, then rethink whether it's a God-given dream. There are so many competing opportunities in our global world right now, but even if your dream carries you into the secular marketplace, you and your dream can still be used to expand the Kingdom of God. God can use you mightily wherever you are. But it's important to think about this question because only what we do for Christ will last. Everything else will be burned up one day and will not matter. Our goal as believers is to live each day as if by nightfall we'll be headed off to heaven. We can't waste time on things that don't matter because, relatively speaking, we don't have long on earth. The Bible says man, "comes forth like a flower and fades away; He flees like a shadow and does not continue." (Job 14:2, NKJV) James says that our lives are we are like "a vapor." So we must live intentionally and make what we do on earth count. In a world where the "selfie" rules, we have to step back and reevaluate whether so much attention

on self and the temporal really matters in the big scheme of things. Jesus said, " If anyone desires to come after Me, let him deny himself, and take up his cross and follow Me." (Matthew 16:24 NKJV) Jesus was about love, compassion and looking after the least, the last and the lost. Ask yourself and deeply consider: Does our dream/vision connect with the broader plan Christ has?

5. How do you plan to implement your dream? Write down three short-term goals on which you will work over the next three months. Start with the goal; target a deadline; and establish a reward for when you've achieved your goal. Make sure each goal is SMART. In other words: specific; measurable; attainable; realistic; and time-sensitive. By setting manageable and SMART short-term goals, you won't get overwhelmed or lose momentum. At the end of the three-month period, note your progress, and then establish three new short-term goals to be completed over the next three months. If at the end of this six-month period, no significant or measurable progress has been made toward your dream or vision, reevaluate, assess your actions and have a talk with God. Are you doing what He wants you to do? Or are you doing it your way?

6. God will speak to you through His Word, so as you read the bible be prepared to listen. As you open your heart to our loving Father, as you ask Him to guide you, He will highlight scriptures related to your dream/vision. God will give you a "rhema" word, a word just for you! Write down the scripture(s), use them as the foundation of your dream to keep you encouraged and grow your faith.

7. Journaling is a good discipline to use when seeking a Word from the Lord. It's also a good tool to use to keep track of

your goals and progress. It can be very beneficial to capture thoughts, ideas and directions you receive from the Lord. Sometimes God will give you a download from Heaven. It's awesome to get revelation straight from the throne.

8. Another tool that can be used is a dream/vision board, which allows you to keep your dream in front of you. In Habakkuk 2:2, NKJV, the writer said, "Write the vision And make it plain on tablets." So to make your own dream/vision board "plain," get a large poster board, trifold board, or cork board and add key words, quotes, scripture, pictures…anything that helps you illustrate your dream and bring it to life. The dream/vision board is your own creation. Have fun with it and make it your own. Focus on who, what, where, how and target dates. As any of these variables change, just update them with new goals. Position your dream board so that it's visible to you every day. There's not a right or wrong way to make a dream/vision board, so if you prefer to create a digital version, make one on your tablet or computer. You can also create a board on Pinterest, but be sure to look at your board daily.

What if you don't feel as if God has revealed a dream/vision to you yet? How do you do the dream/vision work? One thing you can do is spend some time specifically seeking God through prayer and fasting. God will reveal Himself in ways we can't even image.

Another thing to do while waiting for God is to see if there's a vision He's given to someone we already know and trust—and then we can link up with that person's vision. Ask God to show you how to support another's dream/vision. Motivational speaker Zig Ziglar said, "You can have everything in life you want if you will just help enough other people get what they want.." When your desire is to be in the very will of God, it's amazing how things will begin to fall into place. When we give God a total "yes!" things will begin to happen for our good and His glory. Things may not always be perfect, or happen without difficulty, but in the end the vision will come to pass.

Write the Vision/Dream

"Then the Lord answered me and said: 'Write the vision And make it plain on tablets, That he may run who reads it. For the vision is yet for an appointed time; But at the end it will speak, and it will not lie. Though it tarries, wait for it; Because it will surely come, It will not tarry.' ." (Habakkuk 2:2-3, NKJV)

"This will be written for the generation to come, That a people yet to be created may praise the LORD." (Psalm 102:18, NASB)

WHAT: What do you believe one of your BIG God-given dreams is?

WHO: Who do you believe God is calling to help you accomplish this dream/vision?

WHERE: Where will this dream/vision happen?

WHY: Why is this dream important to the Kingdom of God?

HOW: How do you plan to start implementing your dream? (Write down at least three short-term goals to work on over the next three months, include target completion dates, and list reward when you complete a target.)

GOAL	TARGET DATE	REWARD
1.		
2.		
3.		

Add scriptures below that you may use as a foundation for your dream, or that will keep you encouraged.

Things to Remember From Chapter 5

1. When God gives a dream, vision or calling and we hear Him we should write down what He says. (Habakkuk 2:2-3)

2. The vision/dream should be written so it can be easily seen by the person(s) who will carry out the dream. (Habakkuk 2:2-3)

3. As we write down what we believe our God-given vision/dream is, it should be specific. If we don't believe we have heard from God, we may need to connect with someone who has heard clearly from God and help them accomplish what God has said to them.

4. We should write down the names of the people we believe God has assigned to help us accomplish our dream/vision.

5. Determine where we believe God is calling, and what He's is calling us to do. Where you will carry out your dream is very important.

6. Write down why we believe this dream/vision is important to the kingdom of God. God-given dreams have an impact on the Kingdom of God, and not our own kingdom.

7. To launch the dream/vision, we must write down at least three short-term goals to be completed within three months.

8. Write down any scripture God has given you as a foundation for the dream/vision.

9. A dream/vision board may be used to keep the dream in front of us. Words, pictures and goals motivate us to keep pursuing what God has placed within us.

PRAYER

Dear God,

Thank You for the vision You have placed in me. As I write the vision down, I stand with expectation that it will come to pass. I pray that the vision will speak of Your greatness and power. Breathe on the vision and help me to allow the Holy Spirit to power the vision. I will not move in my own strength O God. I submit my vision to the broader vision of the Kingdom expansion. God, allow me to discern who and what needs to be attached to this vision. Let nothing hinder or destroy the vision You have placed in me. Your Word reminds us, "Where there is no vision the people perish." I decree and declare I have a vision and I will not perish!

In Jesus's Name,
Amen.

CHAPTER 6

CREATE A DREAM GIRL NETWORK

Once we articulate our vision/dream and write it down, how do we get it kick started? The best way to get it going is to do it in community. Creating a Dream Group, aka a D-Group, is key to keeping the dream alive and dynamic. A D-Group is a small network of people who nurture and challenge ideas, approaches and actions as we move forward. The D-group is a group of like-minded ladies who commit to come together once a week to give birth to their dreams. It is an accountability group where the women serve as midwives. The group is specifically designed to focus on each other's dreams/vision and encourage each other toward progress. The D-group can provide resources, ideas, recommendations, contacts and much more. The group is to inspire each woman to utilize the skills and gifts she has to accomplish the task at hand. We cannot function as an island unto ourselves. We need other people to offer support and encouragement to develop the plan and ultimately fulfill our God-given dreams. Each group will take on its own personality.

The D-Group is very important. Many times after participants get pumped up from some type of empowerment conference, they lose their enthusiasm because they do not immediately start putting the concepts into practice. The D-Group is meant to keep us focused, on track and accountable. We should let nothing get in the way of our D-Group gathering. In order for the dreams and visions to become reality, we must act on what God is doing. We must not shrink back or become apathetic, for other people's destinies are connected to our dream. It's awesome when we can help and celebrate others and not just focus on ourselves. To have a healthy, vibrant D-Group, members must be fully engaged and present when they meet. A D-group can serve as a very important catalyst to boost your dreams into action. The D-Groups are marked by 6 aims:

1. Encouraging and Serving Each Other

In a world of the "selfie," it has become the norm to look out for self and promote self. Pursuing "my" dream and not worrying about the dreams of others is pretty standard today, but the heart of a D-Group is in encouraging the members of your group as you would want to be encouraged as you work on your vision. It's really not "all about me," it's about encouraging and serving each other as we hear from God. Many times, God uses others to speak into our lives. When we slow down for an hour and a half to listen and hear, it can be refreshing. When we sow our time and self into others, it always comes back—and we will discover that we reaped more than we sowed.

Scripture References: "Therefore encourage one another and build up one another, just as you also are doing." (1 Thessalonians 5:11, NASB). "Finally, brethren, rejoice, be made complete, be comforted, be like-minded, live in peace: and the God of love and peace will be with you." (2 Corinthians 13:11 NASB). "That I may be encouraged together with you while among you, each of us by the other's faith, both yours and mine." (Romans 1:12, NASB). "If your gift is to encourage others, be encouraging, if it is giving, give generously, If God has given you leadership ability, take the responsibility seriously. And if you have a gift for showing kindness to others do it gladly." (Romans 12:8 NLT)

2. Respecting Each Other

God gave us the Golden Rule so that we would know how to respect one another. (Matthew 7:12) Do unto others as you would have them do unto you. Whatever level of respect you want, give that level of respect. For instance, keeping someone's confidence and holding dear what someone has confided in you is a big part of earning someone's respect. Putting someone's business in the street, talking behind a person's back or causing drama of any kind is not respectful. Respect looks like this: I honor you to your face and behind your back. I speak kindly about you when you are not in my presence. I never share anything you shared with me in confidence. I genuinely care about your wellbeing. Disrespect is selfishness on steroids.

Scripture References: "So in everything, do to others what you would have them do to you, for this sums up the law and the prophets." (Matthew 7:12) "Do nothing from selfish or empty conceit, but with humility of mind regarding one another as more important than yourselves. Do not merely look out for your own personal interests, but also for the interests of others." (Philippians 2:3-4, NASB). "Respect everyone, and love the family of believers, Fear God, and respect the king." (I Peter 2:17, NLT). Speaking of leaders the Bible says, "Show them great respect and whole-hearted love because of their work, and live peaceably with each other". (1 Thessalonians 5:13, NLT)

3. Listening to Each Other

Listening is probably the single most important skill you will use in your D-group. In order to understand and give input into another's dream, that must be preceded by careful and compassionate listening. Listening allows for better understanding with clarifying questions and healthy dialogue. Interrupting before someone is finished speaking shows that one is not listening. It's also just plain rude and shows that what you want to say is more important than what the speaker is saying. Relax and listen; everyone will have a chance to talk.

Scripture References: "Listen to the words of the wise; apply your heart to my instruction." (Proverbs 22:18, NLT) "Understand this, my dear brothers and sisters: You must all be quick to listen, slow to speak, and slow to get angry." (James 1:19, NLT) "Anyone with ears to hear should listen and understand!" (Matthew 11:15, NLT)

4. Speaking the Truth in Love

When we have listened for an appropriate amount of time to everyone's issues, then we can take our turn to speak. We must not speak just to avoid the silence. We must speak when we have something significant to say, as prompted by the Holy Spirit. We should see ourselves as a channel flowing with words from God. When we speak, we should speak the oracles of God. Remember, God speaks from a heart of love. Our words must be seasoned with love, and when we give recommendations we should speak the truth in love. The D-group is not for gossip or for getting off on tangents. Our words are very important. The power of life and death is in our tongues. One of the best things we can do for people is to use our voice to speak life into their dreams/visions and calling. Jesus always spoke truth. But please note that what you think to be true is often quite different than speaking the truth in love. Before we speak. we must ask ourselves, what would Jesus say?

Scripture References: "We will speak the truth in love, growing in every way more like Christ, who is the head of his body, the church." (Ephesians 4:15, NLT) "Those who lead blameless lives and do what is right, speaking the truth from sincere hearts. Those who refuse to gossip or harm his neighbors or speak evil of their friends." (Psalms 15:2-3, NLT) Speaking about wisdom, "For I speak the truth and detest every kind of deception. My advice is wholesome. There is nothing devious or crooked in it. My words are plain to anyone with understanding, clear to those with knowledge." (Proverbs 8:7-9, NLT) "I speak with all sincerity; I speak the truth." (Job 33:3, NLT)

5. Praying for Each Other

Never underestimate the power of prayer. Praying is Jesus's full-time job. The Bible says when He went back to heaven after the resurrection, He sat down at the right hand of the Father making intercession for us, (Romans 8:34) which means that He's praying for us right now. Jesus told His disciple Peter He had prayed for Him because Satan wanted to sift Peter as wheat. (Luke 22:31) When a group of people get together and are serious about walking out their purpose and fulfilling every dream/vision God has given them, just know that the devil is mad. But remember: Jesus is praying for us too, and no weapon formed against you will prosper! (Isaiah 54:17) As D-group members share each week, keep their goals and plans in prayer until your next meeting.

Scripture References: "Never stop praying." (I Thessalonians 5:17, NLT). " I pray that from his glorious unlimited resources he will empower you with inner strength through his Spirit." (Ephesian 3:16, NLT). "We always thank God for you and pray for you constantly." (I Thessalonians 1:2, NLT). "I have not stopped thanking God for you. I pray for you constantly, asking God the glorious Father of our Lord Jesus Christ to give you spiritual wisdom." (Ephesians 1:16-17, NLT). "Don't worry about anything; instead pray about everything. Tell God what you need, and thank Him for all He has done. Then you will experience God's peace, which exceeds anything we can understand. His peace will guard your hearts and minds as you live in Christ Jesus." (Philippians 4:6-7, NLT) "We always pray for you, and we give thanks to God, the Father of our Lord Jesus Christ." (Colossians 1:3, NLT)

6. Depending on the Word of God for Direction, Doing the Word of God

The D-group is there for you to receive encouragement, but ultimately the dream is from God and He is the one who gives the direction. The group exists for its members to be cheerleaders, encouragers and supporters. The Word of God is a good measuring rod as to whether the dream is lining up according to kingdom principles. When we hear God's Word, then the next step is to do the Word—to do what it says, or be obedient to the Word. There is no higher source than the Word of God. Jesus came in the flesh as the living Word! When we seek God earnestly about the things that concern Him, He will often give a rhema Word regarding direction, purpose and calling. A rhema word refers to a revealed word that is spoken, when the Holy Spirit delivers a message to the heart.

Scripture Reference: "So prove yourselves doers of the word, and not merely hearers who delude themselves. (James 1:22, NASB) "Every word of God is tested: He is a shield to those who take refuge in Him. (Proverbs 30:5, NASB). Trust in the Lord with all your heart, And do not depend on your own understanding. Seek His will in all you do, and He will show you which path to take." (Proverbs

3:5-6, NLT) "I pondered the direction of my life, and I turned to follow your laws." (Psalm 119:59, NLT)

The *Getting Started: Achieving Your God-Given Dreams Manual* is found in the back of this book. It is a 6-week starter kit to get your D-Group started. Included in the back of this chapter is a group covenant to assure members share the same purpose and group values. The covenant should be signed by all group members at the first meeting.

Things to Remember From Chapter 6

1. The Dream Girl Network is a small group that is a safe place to incubate the dream/vision God has given you and your group members. It serves as a group of midwives to help with a safe delivery of the birthing of the dream.

2. Soon after attending a Dream Girl Weekend Event or reading the I'm A Dream Girl: A Guide to Fulfilling Your God-Given Dreams book, select a small group of like-minded women (4-8 people) to be part of your Dream Group (D-Group). Keep it small and intimate. Too many members will not allow the group to accomplish the goal of sharing and feeling supported.

3. The D-Groups will make their meeting time a priority. They will meet once a week for an hour to an hour-and-a-half. Smaller groups may get by with an hour, but the larger groups will need to meet for one-and-a-half hours to allow for adequate time for each member to share.

4. The D-Group meetings are to be upbeat and inspiring. Each meeting should uplift and encourage all participants. The group must stay on point and adhere to the established goals and ground rules. A group covenant will encourage

authenticity and confidentiality. Have members sign this at the first meeting.

5. The D-Group members will serve, encourage and respect each other. They will also listen to each other, speak the truth in love and pray for one another. (Philippians 2:3-4, 1 Thessalonians 5:11, Romans 12:8, James 1:19, Ephesians 4:15, Ephesians 1:16-17, Philippians 4:6-7)

6. The group will start and end each meeting with prayer.

PRAYER

Heavenly Father,

I am so grateful to You for putting a dream deep within my spirit. I want to move forward and accomplish all that You desire for me. God please reveal to me the people who need to be involved in this vision/dream. Give me the courage to step out and ask for the wisdom to receive the help I need. Enlighten every person who will be part of my Dream Group. Allow my Dream Girl Network to bring glory to You and for each member to be edified. Give each woman the focus necessary to complete the tasks at hand. Allow me to be used in a great way for this generation. Let the kingdom of God be glorified in all that we do.

In Jesus's Name,
Amen.

Dream Group Covenant Agreement

Covenant Purpose

The purpose of the Dream Group (D-Group) Covenant is to insure each member can enjoy and experience an environment of confidentiality, authenticity, fellowship, growth and community. (Ephesians 4:2-3, 29, 32)

Group Values

- **Holy Spirit Led** –The Holy Spirit leads us into all truth. Yielding to the Spirit's lead keeps us on point. (John 16:13)
- **Respect** – Group members must always be cognizant of not embarrassing other group members. (Romans 12:10)
- **Confidentiality** – Issues discussed within the D-Group will not be shared outside of the group. (Proverbs 11:13)
- **Authenticity** – The group must be able to be transparent and share openly among each other. (James 1:26)
- **Active Listening** – In order to understand and give input into another's dream, it must be preceded by careful and compassionate listening. Active listening is the most important skill each group member will use.(James 1:19)
- **Speak Truth in Love** – When speaking to group members, your words should be truthful and seasoned with love. (Ephesians 4:15)

Agreement

Along with the other members of this group, I agree to honor this covenant.

Dream Group Covenant Agreement Signature Page

Please print and sign your name below

Dream Group Members

Print Name	Signature	Date

Group Leader(s)

Print Name	Signature	Date

CHAPTER 7
CLOSING THOUGHTS

God has wonderful and awesome plans for your life! He loves you deeply and wants the very best for you. He has good works for you to walk in, and it's your choice to say "yes" to His plan, or go your own way. You can say "yes" to God at any point you decide—it's never too late. Some of us find our purpose early in life, others find God's plan late in life. Sadly, some people never find God's plan. Our purpose is always connected to the greater purposes of God. His purposes are always motivated by love. When we choose to walk in God's ways, we will find fulfillment that we just won't find in the world.

God's plan for us includes walking in authority and dominion over all that He has for us. Because He made us in His likeness and image, we can walk in dominion and power. God is a spirit and He made us spirits, too. We live in a body while on earth and we possess a soul. Our soul consists of our mind, will and emotions. We are spirit, soul and body. When we come to a saving knowledge of Jesus, He allows our spirits to discern spiritual things. As a result, we're able to tap into our purpose—and God's dreams and visions for us flow when we are led and operated by the Spirit of God who lives in us. Even though we have access to the leading of the Holy Spirit, we don't always chose to. Sometimes we still operate by allowing the mind, will and emotions to take center stage, but this stops our progress on the journey toward our destiny. Many times we don't understand our true identity in Christ, so we live very far under the privileges we have in Him. We are constantly comparing ourselves to our girlfriends, who are carnal at best or maybe even lost in sin. But we must remember that the measuring rod is not our friends and family members…our plumb line is Jesus Christ. God is trying to conform us into the image of Christ. When we allow God to mold and make us after His own will, we find grace and peace. Grace is God's ability to do what we can't do in our own strength. He graces us every day to move through life in love and in His power.

As we walk in grace, we must remember that we have an enemy of our soul who will go to all lengths to thwart God's plans for our lives. We must contend with actual Dream Killers, mental road-blocks the enemy uses to keep us from executing and fulfilling the plans God has for us. Destructive strongholds, fear, procrastination, negative words, unbelief, unhealthy relationships, victim thinking, excuses, busyness and living other people's lives are all Dream Killers. We must have an airtight strategy to deal with the Dream Killers. We must use Godly weapons like prayer, praise, worship, fasting and the Word of God in order to demolish negative strongholds so that we may be the women God created us to be and do the things He created us to do.

As we hear God in the Spirit—or as He speaks to us through His Word in the bible—we must write down the vision/dream He has for us and develop a concrete strategy to assure that God's plan goes forward. One of the best ways to do that is to establish a Dream Group (D-Group). A D-Group is a small group of women who serve as midwives to help usher one another's dreams into the world. They help you push, push, push! And in the process of sharing dreams and goals weekly, the group is accountable to God and each other. Each

D-Group is a part of a larger circle of women in the Dream Girl Network, or DGN. The DGN may be virtual (on-line) or groups who are in the same area who gather periodically to share ideas and encourage one another in the Lord. God does not want us to work in isolation, He wants us to remain together in fellowship because we are His body. The D-Group and the DGN are designed to help us work together to bring God's purposes into the physical realm.

God is tremendously pleased when we function as the Body of Christ, working in unity, moving forward together to expand His Kingdom. Be blessed as you pursue every dream, vision and calling God has for you. I pray you will have sweet dreams every night and that each morning you awaken refreshed in the Lord and ready to achieve God's best for you.

"Satisfy us in the morning with your unfailing love, that we may sing for joy and be glad all our days." (Psalm 90:14, NIV)

PRAYER

Dear God, Thank You for speaking clearly to me about the vision/
dream You have placed inside me. Help me to write down the specifics of that vision and with joyful obedience may I follow wherever You
are leading me. According to Psalm 19:14, NKJV, "Let the words
of my mouth and the meditation of my heart be acceptable in Your
sight, O LORD, my strength and my Redeemer." Send to me the
people You want to be attached to this vision and grant me the dis-
cernment to recognize them, and then guide us so that we may carry
out Your plan and move forward with love, and in grace, power and
dominion. Help me to accept, cherish and nurture the greatness and
potential you have entrusted to me. In the end, let Your vision speak,
let the dream come forth for Your glory. Thank You, O, God!

In Jesus's Name,
Amen.

GETTING STARTED:
ACHIEVING YOUR GOD-GIVEN DREAMS
(6-WEEK STARTER KIT)

INTRODUCTORY PLANNING SESSION

Welcome to the introductory session of the Dream Group, also known as the D-Group! The D-Group members are designed to serve as midwives to help you birth your God-given dream. It is a small network of women who will encourage, empower and draw out your gifts, skills and abilities. Everyone who is born has a purpose. The purpose may be a calling, a dream, a vision or whatever you want to call it. The purpose starts and ends with God. When we are not able to recognize our purpose, apathy, abuse, misuse or neglect have a way of meandering into our lives. When we find purpose, our whole life changes because purpose has a twin, named passion. When purpose and passion work in tandem, great things happen. Passion drives our purpose bus. When we pursue purpose in the context of community, the dream becomes clearer. None of us can function well alone and in isolation. We need each other. People can affirm, challenge and nurture our ideas, approaches and actions as we fulfill our dreams. Ultimately our dreams are placed in us by God. He is pulling for us to pursue the Dream Giver to find out what our destiny is. Destiny does not just happen. We must be engaged and fully on board the purpose bus with the power of passion moving us forward. Affirmation can be helpful as we move on our journey. The D-Group members will not only be midwives but cheerleaders to affirm what God is doing in your life.

Helpful Tips for D-Groups

Commit to coming to the D-Group each week if possible. Make it a priority. What can be more important than pursuing your God-given dream and purpose?

1. Do the work necessary to move toward realizing your dream.
2. Share ideas, contacts, information, feedback and anything that will advance an individual member or the group.
3. Keep the meetings upbeat, enriching and encouraging for the D-Group members.
4. Continue to come to the D-Group regardless of the level of progress you may or may not have made.
5. Be respectful of each other and abide by the ground rules the D-Group decides on.
6. All group meetings are confidential. Information should only be shared by D-Group members.
7. Commit to pray for each person in your D-Group.
8. Read the information in the "Before the Meeting" section prior to coming to the meeting. (It will take only 2-3 minutes.)
9. During the meeting, appoint a timekeeper to allow ample opportunity for each member to speak.
10. Select a time to meet after the 6-weeks for a celebratory gathering to review progress toward dream goals.

OPENING PRAYER:

Dear God, thank You for every dream seed you have planted in me. Please allow the seed planted in good ground to grow, flourish and to provide seed for someone else. Grant us wisdom and insight into our destiny. May we always recognize the dream is not about us but about how we can advance Your kingdom. Let all that we do bring glory to You and not ourselves.

In Jesus's name,

Amen.

Opening Discussion

1. If you participated in a Dream Girl Event and/or read *I'm a Dream Girl: A Guide to Fulfilling Your God-Given Dreams,"* what were your takeaways?

2. Each person, please share your God-given dream. (Include how this dream/vision will advance the Kingdom of God.) If you are not sure of your God-given dream, share what you do (skill, gifting) that other people are blessed by.

3. What do you hope to take away from the D-Group?

Planning for the D-Group Meetings

1. Agree on the following things:
   a. Day of week _____
   b. Time of day_____
   c. Length of the meeting_____ (Best to set the meeting for 1½ hours. If the group finishes early, that

is fine, but do allow for each person to discuss their perspectives.)

    d. Who will facilitate the meeting _____

2. Share Contact information (facilitator can send out information to group)
3. Discuss Dream Group Covenant Agreement and Ground Rules

    a. Confidentiality is a must. Information must not be shared outside the group.

    b. Start and finish meetings on time.

    c. Allow each member time to discuss their perspectives.

    d. All group members sign Dream Group Covenant Agreement.

4. Review Format for upcoming meetings.
5. At the end of the 6-week D-Group, plan a celebratory meeting to acknowledge progress toward realizing God-given dreams.
6. DATE FOR ENDING CELEBRATION

_____

CLOSING PRAYER

Session 1 The Father's Affirmation

Before the Meeting

The Father's love is unconditional. He loves me, period! It is not what I have done or not done but it is about what He has done. He sent His Son to die in my place. He has a wonderful plan for my life. His plan is not to harm me but to give me hope and a future or an expected end. Before I was born, God knew me. He prepared good works for me to walk in during my time on earth. After God made everything, including mankind, He said it was very good. God's original plan was clear; He gave us dominion over all of His creation. He made me in His image. His purpose is to have relationship with me. He loves me and I am to love Him back. He has blessed me, He is blessing me and He will continue to bless me.

Key Scriptures:

Genesis 1-2, Jeremiah 1:5-10, Ephesians 2:10, Jeremiah 29:11, Psalm 139, Jeremiah 31:3

During the Meeting

1. Start the meeting with prayer/invocation or an inspirational story. Feel free to use information from the "Before the Meeting" section.
2. Share something good that has happened to you since the last meeting.
3. What opportunities or challenges (problems) have you experienced since the last meeting? What support would you like this week?
4. Share encouragement, appreciation and acknowledgments

with other members while they press forward.

5. Affirm the Father's love for you and allow that love to push you toward fulfilling your God-given dreams. He is there for you.

Read the Weekly Affirmation together.

Write your own affirmation. (What positive words do you need to tell yourself?)

Framing Your World

Hebrews 11:3, says, "By faith God framed the world with His Word." Since we are made in His image, let's begin to frame our world with our faith-filled words. Life and death are in the power of the tongue. Speak affirming words over the dreams God has given you.

Weekly Affirmation

Long ago the LORD said to Israel: "I have loved you, my people with an everlasting love. With unfailing love I have drawn you to myself.'" (Jeremiah 31:3, NLT)

My Own Affirmation

_____

_____

_____

_____

After the Meeting

Today's Date_____

My goals for this week

1.

2.

3.

CLOSING PRAYER

Note: Review your goals each day and say the affirmations out loud.

SESSION 2 PREGNANT WITH POSSIBILITY

Before the Meeting

In the Old Testament book of 1 Samuel, a woman named Hannah was barren but wanted a child more than anything. She went to the temple and prayed to God for a child so fervently the priest thought she was drunk. Hannah prayed for what God wanted to birth into the earth. The priest prophesied she would become pregnant within the next year. When the baby was delivered, she remembered God's faithfulness and she dedicated the baby to God. After he was weaned, she took the baby to the temple to be raised by the priest as an offering to God. As we ask God to bring forth the dream seeds within us, remember to dedicate them to the Lord and release them back in His care. She named the baby Samuel and he became a great prophet of God and anointed the first two kings of Israel, Saul and David.

Key Scripture:

1 Samuel 1

During the Meeting

1. Start the meeting with prayer/invocation or an inspirational story. Feel free to use information from the "Before the Meeting" section.
2. Share something good that has happened to you since the last meeting.
3. What opportunities or challenges (problems) have you experienced since the last meeting? What support would you like this week?
4. Talk about the progress on the goals from last week.
5. Share encouragement, appreciation and acknowledgments with other group members while they press forward.

6. Affirm that God is able to bring forth the potential and possibilities within you.

Read the Weekly Affirmation together.

Write your own affirmation. (What positive words do you need to tell yourself?)

Framing Your World

Hebrews 11:3 says, "By faith God framed the world with His Word." Since we are made in His image, let's begin to frame our world with our faith-filled words. Life and death are in the power of the tongue. Speak affirming words over the dreams God has given you.

Weekly Affirmation

"For nothing will be impossible with God." (Luke 1:37, NASB)

My Own Affirmation

_____

_____

_____

_____

After the Meeting

Today's Date_____
My goals for this week

1.

2.

3.

CLOSING PRAYER

Note: Review your goals each day and say the affirmations out loud.

SESSION 3 MY IDENTITY IN CHRIST

Before the Meeting

When we come into the revelation of our identity in Christ, freedom is ours! Our relationship with God through Jesus Christ is the cornerstone of our identity. Knowing the truth makes us free. The truth is, we are completely forgiven and fully pleasing to God. We are totally accepted by God. We are deeply loved by God. We are absolutely complete in Christ. When we embrace our new identity in Christ, our purpose becomes clearer. Our self-worth increases when we understand and walk in our identity. It's not what you do as a Christian that determines who you are; it who you are that determines what you do.

Key Scripture:

2 Corinthians 5:17

During the Meeting

1. Start the meeting with prayer/invocation or an inspirational story. Feel free to use information from the "before the meeting" section if you chose to.
2. Share something good that has happened to you since the last meeting.
3. What opportunities or challenges (problems) have you experienced since the last meeting? What support would you like this week?
4. Talk about the progress on the goals from last week.
5. Share encouragement, appreciation and acknowledgments with other group members while they press forward.
6. Affirm that God is making us into a new creation.

Read the Weekly Affirmation together.

Write your own affirmation. (What positive words do you need to tell yourself?)

Framing Your World

Hebrews 11:3 says, "By faith God framed the world with His Word." Since we are made in His image, let's begin to frame our world with our faith-filled words. Life and death are in the power of the tongue. Speak affirming words over the dreams God has given you.

Weekly Affirmation

"...anyone who belongs to Christ has become a new person. The old life is gone; a new life has begun!" (2 Corinthians 5:17. NLT)

My Own Affirmation

_____

_____

_____

_____

After the Meeting

Today's Date_____

My goals for this week

1.

2.

3.

CLOSING PRAYER

Note: Review your goals each day and say the affirmations out loud.

SESSION 4 DEALING WITH BARRIERS

Before the Meeting

In Daniel 3, three young Hebrew men faced challenges because they refused to bow down to an idol in the form of a gold statue. They were thrown into a blazing fire. When asked about their refusal, they said to the king, "We do not need to defend ourselves before you." If you throw us into the furnace, the God whom we serve is able to save us. He will rescue us from your power, but even if He does not, we want to make it clear we will never serve your gods. Even though the furnace was ordered by the king to be seven times hotter, after the men were thrown in, bound, they were walking around in the fire. The king said it looks like four people instead of three in the furnace. The fourth looks like a "God." When we face barriers and seemingly impossible challenges, we can stand on the promises of God, have unwavering faith in God and trust in Him to move through the difficulties. THROUGH is important!! After the men came out of the furnace, not a hair was singed, their clothes were intact and they didn't even smell like smoke. Then they were promoted by the same king who had ordered them into the furnace.

Key Scriptures:

Daniel 3, Psalm 20:7

During the Meeting

1. Start the meeting with prayer/invocation or an inspirational story. Feel free to use information from the "Before the Meeting" section.
2. Share something good that has happened to you since the

last meeting.

3. What opportunities or challenges (problems) have you experienced since the last meeting? What support would you like this week?

4. Talk about the progress on the goals from last week.

5. Share encouragement, appreciation and acknowledgments with other group members while they press forward.

6. Affirm that God can break down and move through barriers.

Read the Weekly Affirmation together.

Write your own affirmation. (What positive words do you need to tell yourself?)

Framing Your World

Hebrews 11:3 says, "By faith God framed the world with His Word." Since we are made in His image, let's begin to frame our world with our faith-filled words. Life and death are in the power of the tongue. Speak affirming words over the dreams God has given you.

Weekly Affirmation

"Some trust in chariots and some in horses, but we trust in the name of the LORD our God." (Psalm 20:7, NIV)

My Own Affirmation

_____

_____

_____

After the Meeting

Today's Date_____

My goals for this week

1.

2.

3.

CLOSING PRAYER

Note: Review your goals each day and say the affirmations out loud.

Session 5 Write the Vision, Do the Vision

Before the Meeting

In the book of Habakkuk, he was instructed to write the vision on tablets and to make it plain so people could run with them. The vision is for the future. Many people put together vision boards, write visions and never do anything about what is written. In order to realize the vision, we must write goals and strategies with timelines. We must not just dream and write the vision, we must also act on what we write. When we put things in writing, it helps us and others remember what God said we are to do. Many times it is for the next generation. Psalm 102:18, NIV, says, "Let this be written for a future generation, that a people not yet created may praise the LORD." The vision is not about us but about fulfilling the purpose for such a time is this. It is to glorify God. He is the reason why we live. "Where there is no vision the people perish…" (Proverbs 29:18, KJV)

Key Scripture:

Proverbs 29:18

During the Meeting

1. Start the meeting with prayer/invocation or an inspirational story. Feel free to use information from the "Before the Meeting" section.
2. Share something good that has happened to you since the last meeting.
3. What opportunities or challenges (problems) have you experienced since the last meeting? What support would you like this week?

4. Talk about the progress on the goal from last week.

5. Share encouragement, appreciation and acknowledgments with other group members while they press forward.

6. Affirm God for the vision and how people flourish with a vision.

Read the Weekly Affirmation together.

Write your own affirmation. (What positive words do you need to tell yourself?)

Framing Your World

11:3 says, "By faith God framed the world with His Word." Since we are made in His image, let's begin to frame our world with our faith-filled words. Life and death are in the power of the tongue. Speak affirming words over the dreams God has given you.

Weekly Affirmation

"Where there is no vision the people perish..." (Proverbs 29:18, KJV)

My Own Affirmation

_____

_____

_____

_____

After the Meeting

Today's Date_____

My goals for this week

1.

2.

3.

CLOSING PRAYER

Note: Review your goals each day and say the affirmations out loud.

SESSION 6 NURTURE THE DREAM IN COMMUNITY

Before the Meeting

When God gives a dream/vision, the birthing of the dream is a process. As with any dream there is the conception, the preparation and the birth. Don't rush the preparation or abort the birth. Incubation of the dream takes time. When it is time for the birth, the midwives are there to help facilitate and guide the process. The D-group members can serve as midwives. When we dream out loud and share the vision/dream in community, the entire community can nurture the dream. During the process and after the process, God deserves the glory. "It's in Christ that we find out who we are and what we are living for. Long before we first heard of Christ…he had his eye on us, had designs on us for glorious living, part of the overall purpose he is working out in everything and in everyone." (Ephesians 1:11, MSG)

Key Scripture:

Ecclesiastes 4:9

During the Meeting

1. Start the meeting with prayer/invocation or an inspirational story. Feel free to use information from the "Before the Meeting" section.
2. Share something good that has happened to you since the last meeting.
3. What opportunities or challenges (problems) have you experienced since the last meeting? What support would you like this week?
4. Talk about the progress on the goals from last week.

5. Share encouragement, appreciation and acknowledgments with other group members while they press forward.
6. Affirm the benefit of working together in community.

Read the Weekly Affirmation together.

Write your own affirmation. (What positive words do you need to tell yourself?)

Framing Your World

Hebrews 11:3 says, "By faith God framed the world with His Word." Since we are made in His image, let's begin to frame our world with our faith-filled words. Life and death are in the power of the tongue. Speak affirming words over the dreams God has given you.

Weekly Affirmation

"Two are better than one, because they have a good return for their labor: If either of them falls down, one can help the other up. But pity anyone who falls and has no one to help them up. Though one may be overpowered, two can defend themselves. A cord of three strands is not quickly broken." (Ecclesiastes 4:9-10, 12 NIV)

My Own Affirmation

_____

_____

_____

After the Meeting

Today's Date_____

My goals for this week

1.

2.

3.

CLOSING PRAYER

Note: Review your goals each day and say the affirmations out loud.

DREAM GROUP LEADER GUIDE

The Dream Group leader is the key to the success of the group. The leader will convene the group and lead the sharing session. Below are helpful tips for the D-Group leader.

1. Review helpful tips from the introductory planning session.

2. Before the session, pray for the participants and the D-Group weekly meeting.

3. Feel free to start the session with information from the "Before the Meeting" section.

4. Ask the Holy Spirit to lead the group and work through you.

5. Assign a timekeeper to assure each person gets an opportunity to share their perspective.

6. Make sure the meeting place is comfortable and without distraction.

7. Find ways to keep group members connected between meetings. Be creative.

8. Lead the discussion, encourage discussion and encourage sharing information to help participants move forward in their dream area.

9. Have group members write 1-3 goals to work on after the meeting and then share their goals.

10. Close the meeting in prayer.

11. At the end of the 6-week session, have a celebratory gathering to acknowledge progress toward the goals. Determine if the group wants to continue.

Notes